Vice Regal Mansions
of
British Columbia

Peter Neive Cotton

Published by
Elgin Publications Ltd.
For the British Columbia Heritage Trust
1981

Acknowledgements

On the death of Peter Cotton in 1979 the manuscript of *Vice Regal Mansions of British Columbia* was left incomplete and preserved in the PABC (Add. Mss. 351). It has been prepared for publication, with the permission of the Provincial Archives of British Columbia, by his friends. The original research and writing commenced in 1958 under the direction of then Provincial Librarian and Archivist, Willard Ireland. Over the years various additions and emendations have been made during unsuccessful attempts to bring the manuscript to publication. In preparing this edition great care has been taken to remain faithful to Peter Cotton's text and support research. Throughout the process the contributions of W. Bassett, Dorothy Blakey-Smith, A. Boyd, D. Denny, Elizabeth Forbes, E. Goodall, W. Halkett, M.C. Holmes, F. Howland, the Hudson's Bay Company, Winnipeg, the late Willard Ireland, Barbara McLennan, Inez Mitchell, Mr. and Mrs. Robert R. Reid, J. Ryan, D.B. Turner, L.J. Wallace, G. Warrington and J.C.S. Wilkinson must be acknowledged. In finally bringing this volume to press we wish to thank in particular Alan Turner, Assistant Deputy Minister, Heritage and Culture, John Bovey, Provincial Archivist and Dr. S.W. Jackman, Professor of History, for their assistance. David Mattison researched the illustrations, reassembled the footnotes and produced the index. Ann West, editorial consultant, has been most helpful in reassembling the manu-script. It has awaited publication some 20 years. The British Columbia Heritage Trust is pleased to finance its publication as the first in a series of monographs on this Province's history and cultural heritage.

MS
Victoria, 1981
for the British Columbia Heritage Trust.

Vice Regal Mansions of British Columbia
Published by Elgin Publications Ltd.
for the British Columbia Heritage Trust
1115 West 64th Avenue
Vancouver, B.C.

Copyright © 1981 British Columbia Heritage Trust

ISBN: 0-9690952-0-2

Typeset in Kennerley Old Style

Design & Manufacture: Scriveners Publication Trades
Vancouver, Canada

Cover: Design – James Bradburne
       Colour Tint – Kiku Hawkes

PRINTED AND BOUND IN CANADA

Contents

List of Illustrations

List of Photographs

Letter of Introduction
by the Lieutenant-Governor

It is perhaps significant that the author of this volume, the late Peter Cotton, began his architectural career in the Department of Public Works. There he specialized in interior design and among his first projects was the interior decor of the new Government House. No doubt this reconstruction, recreating many traditional design elements of the old Government House, inspired the author to proceed along these lines to become British Columbia's first serious restoration architect. Thus the posthumous publication of this 25 year old manuscript is a fitting memorial to his life and work. As one in a one hundred year line of Lieutenant Governors, I can appreciate the social and architectural tradition which this volume explores with both scholarly attention to detail yet popular sense for the 'spirit of the place'.

On behalf of the people of British Columbia I want to congratulate the efforts of the British Columbia Heritage Trust toward finally bringing this informative and stimulating volume to publication.

H.P. Bell-Irving

Governors of British Columbia

COLONY OF VANCOUVER ISLAND
1849-1866

Blanshard, Richard
Governor, 1849-51   Sworn in   March 11, 1850

Douglas, James
Governor, 1851-64   Appointed   May 16, 1851

Kennedy, Arthur Edward
Governor, 1864-66   Sworn in   March 26, 1864

MAINLAND COLONY OF BRITISH COLUMBIA
1858-1866

Douglas, James
Governor, 1858-64   Sworn in   November 19, 1858

Moody, Col. Richard Clement
Lieutenant-Governor   Appointed   September 21, 1858

Seymour, Frederick
Governor, 1864-66   Sworn in   April 21, 1864

UNITED COLONY OF BRITISH COLUMBIA
1866-1871

Seymour, Frederick
Governor, 1866-69   Appointed   October 24, 1866

Musgrave, Anthony
Lieutenant-Governor, 1869   Sworn in   August 23, 1869

Musgrave, Anthony
Governor, 1869-71   Sworn in   January 10, 1870

Lieutenant Governors of British Columbia

Joseph William Trutch	Sworn in	August 14, 1871
Albert Norton Richards	Sworn in	July 28, 1876
Clement Francis Cornwall	Sworn in	July 20, 1881
Hugh Nelson	Sworn in	March 28, 1887
Edgar Dewdney	Sworn in	November 9, 1892
Thomas Robert McInnes	Sworn in	December 1, 1897
Sir Henri Gustave Joly de Lotbinière	Sworn in	June 22, 1900
James Dunsmuir	Sworn in	May 26, 1906
Thomas Wilson Paterson	Sworn in	December 11, 1909
Francis Stillman Barnard	Sworn in	December 17, 1914
Edward Gawler Prior	Sworn in	December 18, 1919
Walter Cameron Nichol	Sworn in	December 25, 1920
Robert Randolph Bruce	Sworn in	February 24, 1926
John William Fordham Johnson	Sworn in	August 1, 1931
Eric Werge Hamber	Sworn in	May 1, 1936
William Culham Woodward	Sworn in	September 5, 1941
Charles Arthur Banks	Sworn in	October 1, 1946
Clarence Wallace	Sworn in	October 2, 1950
Frank Mackenzie Ross	Sworn in	October 3, 1955
George Randolph Pearkes	Sworn in	October 13, 1960
John Robert Nicholson	Sworn in	July 2, 1968
Walter Stewart Owen	Sworn in	March 19, 1973
Henry Bell-Irving	Sworn in	May 18, 1978

Disputed Territory
OF
COLUMBIA
OR
OREGON,
Showing its Limits
AS SETTLED BY DIFFERENT TREATIES,
and the Boundaries proposed by
ENGLAND & AMERICA.

From the Large Map of M. Duflot de Mofras
and other recent & authentic sources

NOTES ON OREGON
Extent of Country Length 650 Eng. Miles average breadth 550 M
Area 360.000 Sq M or 3 times greater than the British Islands
Population Indian Tribes & settlers 15.000 to 20.000
Produce Timber Fish & Peltry. Few places fit for Cultivation
Settlements Chiefly Forts or Posts of the Hudson Bay & N W Fur Co's
Missions Stations & settlements of Americans & French Canadians
Navigation The Columbia R. discovered by Heceta 1775, is accessible
only during a portion of the year, & navigation is impeded by
rapids at about 100 M from its mouth Excellent harbours N.
of the Columbia but none good to the S. between it & C. Mendocino

TREATIES
By the Convention of 1818 renewed 1827 the country W of the Rocky M's
is open to the subjects of England & America In 1824 & again in 1826
England proposed the Columbia R. as a boundary of partition
America proposed the 49th parallel of Latitude In 1826 modifications
of these were proposed, but not accepted The Convention of 1818 is still
in operation, and may be terminated by either party on giving
12 Months notice.

CHAPTER ONE

Under the Hammer

IN THE SIXTH YEAR OF THE REIGN OF QUEEN VICTORIA the Governor and Company of Adventurers of England trading into Hudson's Bay established Fort Victoria in the harbour of Camosun. The time was 1843 and the Company was in its 173rd year.

At this time, the boundary between British and American possessions west of the Rocky Mountains was undetermined. The Hudson's Bay Company virtually represented Britain in this "Oregon country". Their district was named the "Columbia Department" after the Columbia River on which they had built their headquarters, Fort Vancouver. The Company were protected by their exclusive 'License of Trade' with the Indians insofar as British subjects were concerned, but the American immigrants were under no such restriction; the increasing pressure of the Americans impelled the Company to prepare an alternate position more secure from interference.

In 1846, the signers of the Oregon Boundary Treaty accepted the forty-ninth parallel as the boundary, and the Company headquarters was definitely on American soil. In the Treaty negotiations the British claims had not been strongly pressed, but a fortuitous concession of the whole of Vancouver's Island to the Crown left Fort Victoria British. The Treaty permitted the Company to maintain their forts and trade in American territory but the Cayuse War—an Indian uprising in the Columbia Valley—imperilled their lines of communication and so, on order from England, the headquarters of the Columbia Department was shifted to Fort Victoria.

Great Britain recognized the urgency of colonizing her newly defined territory as a counterpoise to the effective American occupation of the Oregon Territory. Thus, the Colonial Office reluctantly accepted a proposal for the colonization of Vancouver's Island under the auspices of the Hudson's

Bay Company. By Royal Grant, dated 19 January 1849, the whole of the island was transferred to the Company on the condition that settlements be established there.

Initially the Secretary of State for the Colonies, Earl Grey, was prepared to allow the Company the selection of the first Governor of the colony. Their choice fell on James Douglas, Chief Factor in charge of Fort Victoria and a veteran of the western fur trade service. However, there was already a growing dissatisfaction with the monopolistic privileges enjoyed by the Company and, in the face of public criticism of the appointment of a "Company man" as Governor, the decision was reversed and Richard Blanshard, an obscure young English barrister with no experience in the Colonial Service, received his commission as Governor on 16 July 1849.

Rarely had a colonial governor accepted appointment under less propitious conditions. No salary was attached to the office, but Blanshard believed he was to receive a grant of 1000 acres of land. Actually, the intention of the Colonial Office was that he should receive only the revenue from a reserve of 1000 acres, a revenue which, during his tenure of office, amounted to nothing. Moreover, he was dependent for his maintenance upon supplies provided him by the Hudson's Bay Company at three hundred per cent over prime cost. There were few colonists to govern and, as most of them had affiliations with the Company, they turned more to the Chief Factor than to the Governor for guidance.

Shortly after the appointment of Blanshard, Archibald Barclay, Secretary to the Hudson's Bay Company in London, wrote to Douglas informing him of the situation:

Mr. Richard Blanshard, a gentleman of great intelligence and respectability... is to have a grant of land to the extent of 1000 Acres, as he may require it. This grant is not made to him as an individual but in his public capacity and will always belong to the Governor for the time being. You and he together will select some eligible spot....

A house will also have to be provided for him but a very temporary one will answer the purpose for the present and until funds arise from the Sale of land and other property.[1]

This letter reached Douglas only two weeks before Blanshard himself arrived in H.M.S. *Driver* 10 March, 1850.

> ...on the 11th I landed and read my commission in presence of Commander Johnson of H.M.S. "Driver" and the officers and servants of the Hudson's Bay Company; no lodging being ready for me I have been compelled to remain on board the "Driver" during her stay in the Colony...I should wish for a further direction on this point.[2]

The *Driver* could not remain indefinitely to provide accommodation for the Governor and, on the ship's departure on 9 April, Blanshard was given a room in the Fort.

Slowly the work on his house went ahead—too slowly for Blanshard's liking. On 26 June he wrote to Douglas:

> I find that the labourers who for the last few days have been employed on the cottage which has been commenced for my residence have again been withdrawn.
>
> During the four months I have been in this colony the work at the cottage has been totally discontinued with the exception of a few days when labourers varying in number from one to three have been employed.
>
> I request that you, as representative of the Hudson's Bay Company in the colony will inform me whether it is the intention of that Company to supply proper labour to complete the work at the cottage, which I was informed by the Directors I should find ready on my arrival, or whether I am no longer to rely on their doing so.

Subsequently, on August 5 he returned to the subject:

> I find that the three of the Kanakas (Hawaiians— then known also as Sandwich Islanders) and one of the workmen have been withdrawn from my cottage, leaving one solitary man to carry on work that has already been loitered over for more than five months. I beg to state that you are at liberty to withdraw him also, as the labour of a single man is a mere mockery and I will consider such withdrawal as proof of the inability or unwillingness of the Hudson's Bay Company to furnish me with lodging.

There is no copy available of Douglas' answers to Blanshard, but he did discuss the situation freely in a letter to Barclay on 10 September:

> I herewith transmit copies of correspondence with Governor Blanshard relative to the dwelling house I was directed to put up for him at this place.
>
> We have done every thing in our power to forward the building; but unfortunately it was impossible, with our limited means to keep pace with his wishes; without altogether neglecting the Company's business and making it a secondary object, or hiring Mechanics in the Columbia at the enormous rates there for labour, and I did not feel at liberty to adopt either of these expedients....
>
> The house is now nearly finished and he will soon move into it; so that there will be an end of trouble, from that source. The size of the Governor's House is 40 x 20 ft, with a kitchen 18 x 12 feet attached and a house 24 x 18 for his servants. The house is ceiled and painted inside. It has a neat appearance and is on the whole the best finished building in Oregon.
>
> I beg to recommend in the event of any other public buildings being contemplated, that Mechanics may be sent out to erect and finish them, as we have not a single house carpenter or Joiner at this place, our own work being done by the rude self-taught carpenters of the country, who are not capable of turning out a neat job.

Both men were in an unenviable situation. Possibly with a view to clarifying their relative positions the Secretary of the Company wrote to Blanshard early in 1851:

---

1. Barclay to Douglas, Douglas correspondence, 3 Aug. 1849.
2. Blanshard to Grey, Blanshard despatches, 8 Apr. 1850.

The Governor and Committee would recommend that a moderate sized but respectable house and premises should be erected as the official residence for yourself as Governor, calculated for the commencement of the Colony, rather than for what you may anticipate it may come to in time, as the funds that can be relied upon are limited and small at present. . . .

The site of these buildings should be near the Fort Victoria for convenience and protection, and the materials should be stone as preferable to wood to diminish the risk of fire. . . .[3]

By the time this letter reached him, Blanshard, fully convinced of the untenable nature of his position and plagued by ill-health, had already submitted his resignation to the Colonial Secretary. After holding office for only eighteen months Blanshard left the colony early in September 1851, a sadly disillusioned and considerably less wealthy man.

The Governor's house had originally cost $1,548.55 but Blanshard had carried out $684.90 of further improvements for which he was reimbursed prior to his departure for England. For a short time after the Governor's departure, Dr. J.S. Helmcken and his bride were permitted to "live in Government House—i.e. Governor Blanshard's house formerly". In his reminiscences, written years later, Helmcken describes it as "only a four room building on about four lots; faced with planed shingles. It was comfortable but not commodious. . ." Still later he noted that it had "two rooms and a kitchen, with mighty little furniture—but quite enough for two. . ." Richard Colledge, the new Governor's private secretary, he noted "found a sleeping place in the house somewhere".[4]

This is almost the last reference to the building as Blanshard's residence. It became known as "Government House", and Douglas seems to have used the building as his office, although he did receive visitors and transact business in his own home. On this subject, John Pelly, Governor of the Hudson's Bay Company, had written to Douglas on 23 May 1851:

With respect to the House built for the Governor which you say stands on part of the Fur Trade lands, the fur trade may retain it on paying the expense of erecting it and another house may be built for the Governor.

Nevertheless, for some reason of his own, perhaps his sense of economy, Douglas never took advantage of this offer.

Helmcken clearly indicated the house as being at the corner of Yates and Government Streets. The accompanying maps* show the position of the house and grounds in 1851 and again in 1858. Both indicate the lack of alignment with the surveyed streets. The earlier map has already appeared in an article in the *Beaver* on the memoirs written in 1925 by James Robert Anderson, who was a boy of nine when he arrived in Fort Victoria in 1850. Looking back on those early days he said: "Outside the fort yard, to the northward of the eastern gate along the line of Government Street, stood the bake shop and residence, during his short stay, of Governor Blanshard."[5]

It is puzzling to ascertain which structure Anderson referred to as the residence of Governor Blanshard. Other evidence refers to the bake shop as being on the corner of Fort and Government Streets; so the other structure (shown on the Fort Plan on the opposite side of Government to the Fort) must be what Blanshard referred to as "small log hut at Victoria, which was handed over to [E.E. Langford], in which he put away his family in the best way that he could. . . . I suppose [it was] about 20 feet by 12. . . containing one [room]. . . .

he had a large family, and his wife, who was a most lady-like woman, was within a day or two of her confinement, and I gave them rooms in my house, being extremely sorry to see an English lady

3. Barclay to Blanshard, Blanshard correspondence, 1 Jan. 1851.
4. Helmcken, reminiscences, v. 3, 1892.
5. J.R. Anderson, Notes and comments on early days and events in British Columbia. . ., [1925].

*Editor's Note: One map missing from original text. Passage retained for descriptive value.

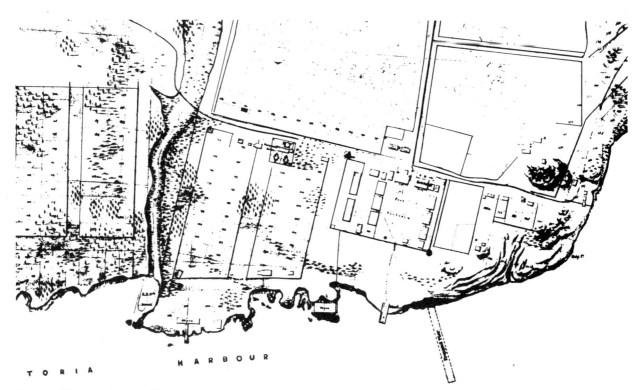

Figure 2: Victoria showing "Governor's House," the bake shop and Langford's hut, 1857. Hudson's Bay Company Archives, Provincial Archives of Manitoba.

reduced to such a state of inconvenience... he was a distant connexion of mine."[6]

Presumably it was after her confinement that the Langford family occupied the log hut while awaiting the completion of their home at Colwood. This provided young Anderson with this story:

> The first piano ever seen in Victoria, or indeed in the whole of the present British Columbia, was brought by Mr. Langford, and as may be imagined great was the curiosity to hear it played and many an idle moment I spent outside of the Langford residence just outside the Fort near the bakery where they were housed when they arrived and before they went to the farm at Colwood.

This is probably the origin of the idea in Anderson's mind that since Blanshard was related to Langford, and had given him shelter, the house in which the Langfords lived after Blanshard left had been Blanshard's own house. The actual building which we

now know to be Blanshard's house, Anderson refers to as having been erected by Douglas:

> ...shortly after Blanshard's relinquishment of his position as Governor... Mr. Douglas was appointed and a second stockaded Fort of small dimensions enclosing his official residence and office was constructed to the north of the existing Fort and some fifty or seventy-five yards distant. There with Mr. Richard Colledge as his Secretary, he carried on the affairs of state.

For the next eight years there is little mention of "Government House" other than as a letter heading. On 25 June 1858, Victoria's first newspaper, the *Victoria Gazette,* started publication in the old Hudson's Bay Company salmon storehouse within the Fort. This was an indication of a transformation that was beginning. Victoria had suddenly received a transfusion in the form of thousands of miners coming in response to rumours of gold finds in the Fraser River. Discoveries of gold prompted the formation of the mainland Colony of British Columbia. The resulting population growth

6. Great Britain, Parliament, House of Commons, Select Committee on the Hudson's Bay Company, *Report, 1857.*

was reflected in the added duties and enlarged staff of the administration.

Amongst the plans in the Archives of British Columbia is one showing a projected scheme for the enlargement of Government House to provide more office space. Douglas, however, had another grander plan:

...for building the various Government offices and residences on the Indian Reserve near James Bay and selling the Government land near the Fort to defray the expenses.[7]

7. Vancouver Island, Legislative Council, *Minutes,* 1851-61, 1918.

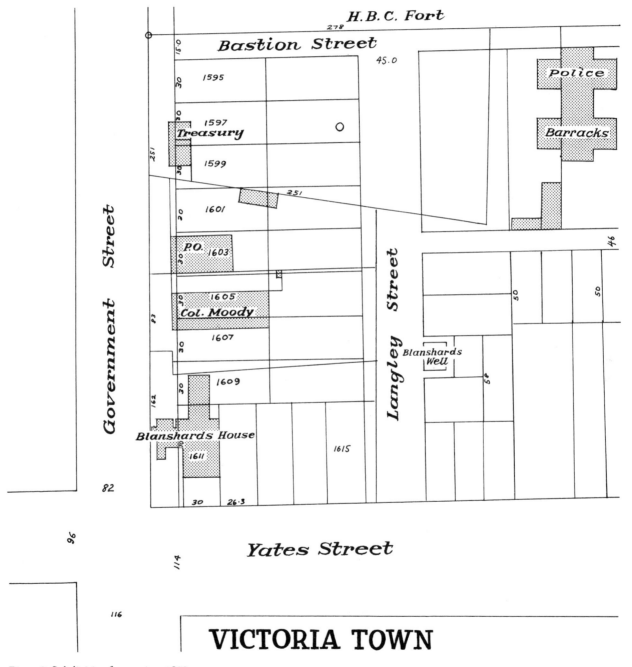

Figure 3: Subdivision for auction, 1859.

Apparently the projected scheme of additions to Blanshard's house did not provide enough offices and the site limited further expansion. Another consideration was the expense involved: by selling the more valuable town lots and using the proceeds for buildings on cheaper land, the Governor could provide more accommodation for the same outlay of money. Douglas took the initiative and implemented this plan but the newly-formed Assembly took exception to this "unconstitutional... breach of privilege."[8] Douglas, however, pressed on and proceeded with the plan. On 3 May 1859, the whole block was auctioned and Donald Fraser paid $130.00 for Blanshard's house and $3,100.00 for the 30' x 70' lot (No. 1511) on which it sat. The conditions of sale called for the purchasers to remove the structures at one week's notice. When or where Fraser removed the Governor's house is still unknown. Subsequently the site became that of the Adelphi saloon; later the Adelphi Block. Today the Post Office occupies the site.

In 1851 Douglas had built his own house on the southern shore of James Bay and although authorized to build another house for the Governor he never did, using his private house as the official residence. Governor Douglas' house was built just after Blanshard's was completed and, unfortunately, there is little information concerning its construction. When Dr. Helmcken married the Governor's daughter, Cecelia, Douglas prevailed upon him to build next door. The difficulties encountered by Dr. Helmcken in the erection of his home were probably typical of those to be encountered everywhere on Vancouver Island—long and frequent delays, shortages of men and materials—all perhaps explain in part the exasperating slowness of building Blanshard's house.

... There were no contractors, everything had to be done piecemeal. There being no lumber it had to be built with logs squared on two sides and six inches thick. The sills and uprights were very heavy and morticed—the supports of the floor likewise—the logs had to be let into grooves in the uprights.

Well the timber had to be taken from the forest—squared there and brought down by water. All this had to be contracted for by French Canadians, then when brought to the beach—I had to beg big oxen of the Company to haul it to the site. Then other Canadians took on the job of putting the building up as far as the logs were concerned—and then shingling—the indians at this time made shingles—all split. All this was very heavy very expensive and very slow work, for the men were by no means in a hurry... They chiefly took their pay in blankets and provisions and other ectas {i.e. ik-tahs, meaning 'goods'}—the balance in coin.

Well the shell is up—now to get it finished—lumber very scarce and a favour to get any at forty dollars per thousand in the rough—so it all had to be planed and grooved by hand! Much of it was cut by Kanakas in a saw pit—so it was not very regular

Figure 4: H.O. Tiedeman plan of proposed additions to the Blanshard house, 1859.

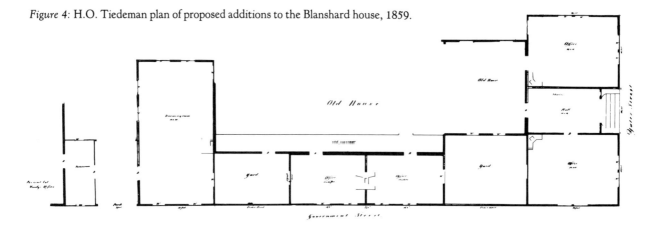

8. Vancouver Island, House of Assembly, *Correspondence,* 1856-59, 1918.

thickness. He had a yellow cedar planking for doors, windows, and skirting boards sent down to him from Fort Rupert.

It is reasonable to assume that Governor Douglas' own residence had as slow and wearing a growth as Helmcken describes. The site was choice. The ground sloped down from the house to the water's edge of James Bay. The 1861 assessment roll shows land at £4,000 and improvements at £10,950. The assessment roll of the next year shows it to be Sec. VI of 11 acres assessed at £38,000.00 and in 1868, after Douglas had subdivided part of his land, the property is assessed at £6,500, and the improvements at £2,000. The drop in value reflects the depression in the colonies after the gold rush was

Figure 6: Cover of 1902 Auction Catalogue.

misconception.

5ᵗʰ On the 1ˢᵗ January 1851 the Hudson Bay Company acquainted Governor Blanshard that the sum of £4000 would be placed at his disposal for the erection of some of the Buildings most urgently required, and informed him that those Buildings, "and the lands that may be appropriated with them" were to be held by him and his Council as Trustees "for the Colony", and further that the site of these buildings should be near Fort Victoria for convenience and protection".

6ᵗʰ For the better information of your Grace I enclose a copy a copy of the entire Despatch in which the above instructions are embodied. —

7ᵗʰ Shortly after the receipt of these instructions Governor Blanshard left the Colony, but a residence for the Governor was put up before his departure, and this very Building with the land appropriated to it was that sold in May last, and was claimed by Mr Berens on behalf of the Hudson Bay Company.

8ᵗʰ I became Governor Blanshard's immed= =iate successor and carried out so far as I was able the other arrangements contemplated by the Hudson Bay Company.

The land appropriated to the Government House was always regarded by me as a Government reserve and the Colonial Surveyor had strict orders from me not to dispose of any part thereof, and

Figure 5: 1860 *Letter-book* facsimile. Douglas to Duke of Newcastle.

over. Apparently the house itself was a Quebecois house type, a rectangular two-storey building with an attic. The main floor seems to have been bisected by a wide hall, with dining and breakfast room on one side (and presumably kitchen services). On the other side were a front and a back drawing room and, upstairs, another hall and at least three bedrooms.

After Douglas' death, the house suffered the same fate as the Blanshard house. In 1902 the furniture was auctioned off and four years later, on 4 October 1906, the house itself was sold by auction. The passing of one of the oldest houses in Western Canada almost slipped by unremarked but for two small notices of the sale in the Victoria *Colonist* and *Times.*

---

9. Helmcken, reminiscences, v. 3.

GOVERNMENT STREET, BEFORE THE REMOVAL OF THE "OLD BASTION."

The above view of Government street was taken a short time previous to the removal of its most prominent feature—the Old Bastion—located at the eastern angle of the stockade of the H. B. Co.'s Fort. That obstruction has since been taken away from the line of the street, leaving a clear sidewalk on the west side.

West of the enclosure is a small building erected since the "Fraser fever" populated the town, and used as a Post Office and Custom House. The house next to it, originally designed for the purpose indicated by the sign over the porch, has been somewhat altered, and is now occupied as a residence by Lieut. Gov. Moody and family.

On the opposite side of the street several changes have taken place since the foregoing was placed in the hands of the engraver, which, while they do not detract from the accuracy of the picture at the time it was taken, render it less perfect in detail than if its characteristics were brought down to the present writing. The principal buildings on this side of the street at this time, are the Colonial Restaurant, Metropolitan Hotel, residence of Capt. Dodd, (of the H. B. Co.,) the large building of Capt. Stamp, the store of Wm. B. Smith, Esq., and the Hotel de France ; while in the distance, on the same side, may be seen the Victoria Hotel, the first brick building erected in Victoria.

PUBLISHED AT THE OFFICE OF THE VICTORIA GAZETTE

Figure 7: Victoria *Gazette* engraving of Government Street, 1859.

CHAPTER TWO

Cottage Without Pretensions

WHEN SIR EDWARD BULWER LYTTON, SECRE-
tary of State for the Colonies, decided to
supply Douglas with assistants for the new colony
of British Columbia he chose the men with care.
Colonel Richard Clement Moody, commanding a
detachment of Royal Engineers, was one such man.
Lytton entrusted to him the selection of a capital
city site. Attention had to be paid to military considerations, city layout and the provision, through
the specially chosen tradesmen, of the necessary
skills for a pioneer community. Moody arrived in
Victoria on 25 December 1858, "not in time, I regret
to say," writes Douglas:

> to take part in our Christmas festivities, which
> would have been all the gayer for his presence. Our
> quarters are rather crowded at this moment, in con-
> sequence of so many official arrivals, and the want of
> official residences, but we have contrived through
> the kindness of friends to procure temporary house
> accommodation for the whole party.[1]

Moody's family planned to stay in Victoria until
he had quarters prepared for them at the new
capital. Moody held a dormant commission as
Lieutenant-Governor of British Columbia, in case
Douglas was incapacitated. The fact that it was
dormant was at this time either unknown to, or
ignored by, Douglas. However, Douglas treated
Moody as his Deputy and wrote the letter quoted.
The letter is interesting because it was written by
the Governor of Vancouver Island from the first
building to be built as a Government House for that
colony and gives instructions for the housing of the
first Lieutenant-Governor in what might be regarded
as the first Government House of British Columbia.

The building in which Moody and his family lived
in Victoria – "a very tiny house full of my dear
Children" – had been intended for the constabulary.[2]
New police barracks and court rooms had been
built in the fall of 1858 on Bastion Square (replaced
in 1889 by the building which still stands). The
renovations to the original 25' x 60' building cost
196/19/0 pounds.

On 4 January 1859, Moody was sworn into office
and left the next day for the Fraser River on his
first visit to the mainland. For military reasons,
Moody decided that Langley, at that time the principal settlement in the Colony, was a poor location
for the capital since it was on the "American" bank
of the river and he proceeded to choose the site
that was to become New Westminster. The Royal
Engineers made their camp, which they called
'North Camp', north-east of the town, round a bend
in the river from "Queensborough" (as the capital
was first called), and to this camp Moody brought
his family on 16 May 1859.

Moody had already spent considerable time at
the camp before he moved his family, and had, in
February, written to Douglas for authority to build
several buildings including a residence for the
Lieutenant-Governor. The first report of construction is in the Victoria *Gazette* of 7 April 1859, which
refers to "one or two temporary buildings having
been already built for the accommodation of Lieut.
Gov. Moody and suite." A letter from Judge
Matthew Baillie Begbie to Douglas, on 12 March
1859, reports that "the men are in a log hut & the
Colonel in a shake house". Arthur T. Bushby's
diary of the same day mentions that

> as yet there are only two wooden huts there one for
> Col. Moody & the other for the men – what a glori-
> ous sight the downright wooden log hut, a fireplace

---

1. Douglas to Blackwood, Douglas correspondence, 27 Dec.
1858.

2. *British Columbia Historical Quarterly,* Jan.-Apr. 1951, p. 107.

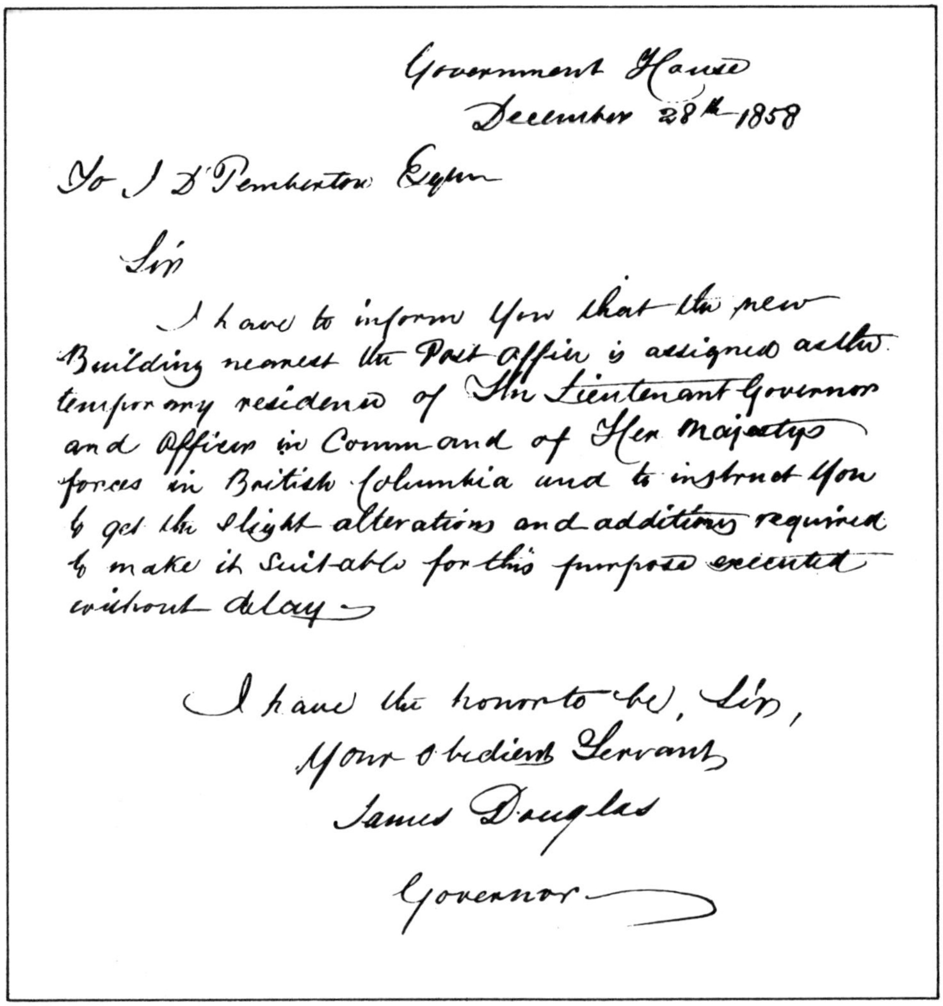

Government House
December 28th 1858

To J D Pemberton Esqre

Sir

I have to inform You that the new Building nearest the Post Office is assigned as the temporary residence of the Lieutenant Governor and Officer in Command of Her Majestys forces in British Columbia and to instruct You to get the slight alterations and additions required to make it suitable for this purpose executed without delay —

I have the honor to be, Sir,
Your obedient Servant
James Douglas
Governor

Figure 8: Facsimile of Douglas letter, 1858, from "Douglas Correspondence Outward".

> big enough to roast an ox & such a fire – logs too big for me to lift... shook down our blankets in the corner of the hut as best we could.[3]

However, such accommodation was obviously inadequate for Moody's family and, on 9 May 1859, Moody wrote Douglas the first of a fascinating series of letters between the Governor and his "Lieutenant-Governor Commander of the Troops & Commissioner of Lands & Works for British Columbia":

> It is due to your Excellency as well as to myself to draw your attention to the necessity of my constructing at once at the Capital of B. Columbia a House proper for the reception of myself and Family.
>
> Yr. Excellency is aware of the manner in which we have borne the great discomfort of our position from the date of my arrival in the country – a period of nearly five months. I know your Excellency's disposition to aid us in every way and I was unwilling that expenditure should be incurred on my account for an arrangement that could only be temporary.
>
> The time however has now arrived when a proper permanent arrangement and a suitable residence has become an indispensable necessity.
>
> I consider the sum of 1000 pounds would be sufficient for the present leaving supplementary additions to be furnished from time to time hereafter.

3. Quoted from original in possession of New Westminster Historic Centre according to Cotton ms.

Douglas replied on 16 May 1859:

> In reply . . . I feel it is unnecessary for me to impress upon you how anxious I am to take any step in my power that might add to the respect due to your Honor, or that might conduce to your own personal comfort; but your Honor is well aware of the difficult situation in which I am at present placed. The expenditure of the Colony is now exceeding the income, and I am not allowed to obtain assistance from the Home Government except to enable me to meet the expenses incurred on Military Account. All other disbursements must be met from Colonial Funds; and the amount of Colonial Funds now in the Chest is at this moment scarcely sufficient to defray outstanding liabilities.
>
> Under these circumstances I can hardly doubt that your Honor will agree with me as to the propriety, as well as the expedience, of deferring any action in the matter until after the Sale of Town Lots at Queensborough.

By the time Moody received this letter his family had arrived at New Westminster, and he replied to the Governor on 18 May 1859:

> I trust your Excellency knows me too well and judging by the past 5 months will not attribute to me undue impatience.
>
> You also I am sure give me credit for entering most thoroughly into all your anxieties respecting the revenue and the expenditure. I also feel assured of Your Excellency's kindness to my family and myself personally as well as your desire to uphold me rightly in my official position. These points I believe are all so clear that they scarcely need to be alluded to—I only recall them to you to try to give ease to your Excellency's mind in a matter concerning myself as I would on all occasions be to you a source of comfort and support and never the contrary.
>
> In this particular matter permit me to say to your Excellency that the accommodation now about to be used by us at the Camp consists of a very small cottage—the quarters of an officer who has been (and still is) under canvass [sic] from the middle of winter—just sufficient to house my children and to cook under cover—My wife, I and servants will be in tents—I have been very scrupulous in postponing to the last providing quarters for myself or for my Officers—I am providing first for the Soldiers' wives & children and the sick, then for the Soldiers themselves to get them out of crowded tents as soon as we can—The Officers and myself will literally be the last provided for, an example I trust which will be productive of good in many ways—We make no complaint—we feel assured of Your Excellency's favourable consideration and kindness toward us.
>
> I have made . . . enquiries . . . which give me ample reason to believe the receipts from the sales of town-lots in Queensborough, Douglas, Yale & Hope . . . will reach an amount fully to justify your Excellency in authorizing me at once to give orders for the construction of my House . . .
>
> I would finally observe I propose to construct what in England would be considered a cottage with Bedrooms in the roof and which could be erected there for a small sum—a House *not* appropriate to my position in a Colony of such consequence—as we all hope this will become but suitable in some degree to its present state—I will take care to design it however in such a manner that it can be further improved and added to some future day.

The next day, Douglas gave Moody permission to expend 1,000 and proceed with construction.

This was good news. Immediately, on 20 May, Moody wrote and thanked Douglas and, possibly, began building at that time, but in the next letter from Douglas there was a marked change of tone. Douglas had had a letter from Sir Edward Bulwer Lytton pointing out:

> an inaccuracy into which you have fallen . . . in designating Colonel Moody the Lieutenant-Governor: you will observe that it is of importance to bear this in mind as his functions in this capacity will commence only in the event of the death or absence of the Governor.

As a result the next letter from Douglas to Moody, on 7 July 1859, was somewhat less encouraging:

> . . . as Her Majesty's Government refuse to recognize such a Functionary (as a Lieutenant-Governor) except he be administering the Government, I think it right, to prevent any misunderstanding, now to

NORTH ELEVATION.

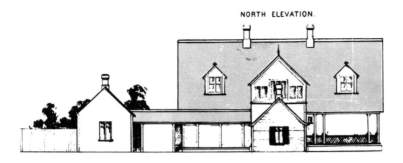

WEST ELEVATION.   SOUTH ELEVATION.

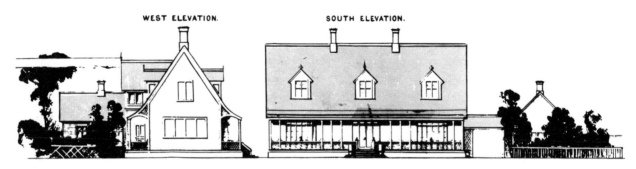

Figure 9: Elevations of the New Westminster Government House, 1860.

SECTION OF STAIR CASE.   UPPER FLOOR PLAN.

GROUND PLAN.

SECTION.

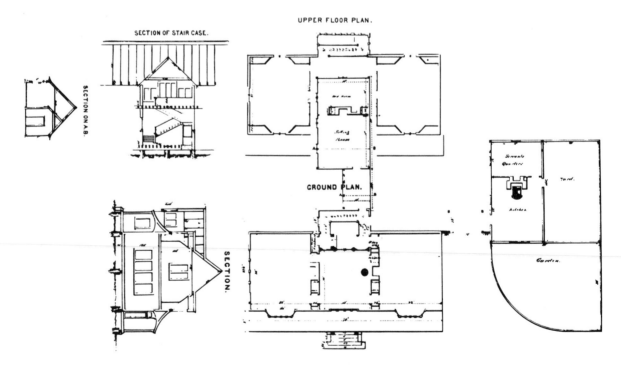

Figure 10: Floorplan of the New Westminster Government House, 1860.

request that you consider the House, so to be erected, as the *Government House* at Queensborough, and not specially as the Residence of the Lieutenant-Governor, the permission to construct such a residence having been granted under an impression which Her Majesty's Government have pointed out to be erroneous.

In expending the amount I have sanctioned I feel I need scarcely beg you to be scrupulously exact that the sum be not, in any way exceeded, even by a labor employed beforehand or otherwise, and considering the depressed state of the finances of the Colony and the heavy expenses for the Royal Engineers which we are called upon to meet, I trust it may be in your power to erect such a Building as may answer all necessary purposes at present at a Sum even considerably under One Thousand pounds.

No direct reply to this letter appears to have survived; the next communication from Moody to Douglas in reference to the house is dated a full two months later. There is a letter from Moody to Captain W.D. Gosset, Treasurer of British Columbia, on 25 August 1859, asking that he pay 200 pounds due to the contractor

according to the terms of a contract entered into with him for the erection of a Government House at New Westminster for which you have received an Advance Warrant from His Excellency the Governor for the sum of One thousand pounds and have already paid Four hundred pounds out of that sum.[4]

The contractor, a Mr. Kells, had done some other work around New Westminster for the Government, but proved to be an unreliable risk to his creditors. Neither the specifications nor the agreement for this structure is in the Archives. This may be accounted for by a letter from the Auditor-General, W.A.G. Young, on 16 August 1861, asking Moody for his annual returns of work finished, and in progress, for the years 1859 and 1860. It is curious that he should have been allowed to let his reports get so far in arrears. If Moody had begun to build on the first notice of sanction from Douglas (i.e. the

last week in May) he would have had over three months in which to build a house, and it certainly appears that he did build since he wrote to Douglas on 8 September 1859:

I shall feel greatly obliged by your Excellency conveying to me a sanction for the occupation of the house constructed for me at the Camp at New Westminster. I mean a sanction to occupy it during the period I propose to remain in the Colony.

Your Excellency may remember a letter (7 July) being addressed to me in some degree altering the conditions as to its appropriation and desiring that it be considered Government House. I have made sundry alterations from the original design in consequence of your order respecting the cost, and it is now certainly at least not more than what the position I have the honor to fill fully entitles me to expect. At the same time it is my duty to submit it is not adapted to the appropriation you wish, nor worthy of it in any way....

The original letter is endorsed in pencil: "Such authority to b' granted. J.D.", and below this is a draft of a letter saying that "... the House should be permanently occupied by you, and I therefore approve of its being considered the Residence of the Colonel Commandant of the Troops." It must then have been this house of which Admiral R.L. Baynes writes in a letter to his wife (then at Valparaiso) on October 6, 1859: "Col. M has built himself an excellent house, one, if it were of Brick instead of wood, I should have no objection to in England."[5] But the editor of the *New Westminster Times* on 11 October 1859, speaks of it rather bitterly as "an extravagantly expensive residence for the Chief Commissioner." Colonel Moody, however, was still not satisfied that the building he had erected was good enough for a Government House. In his letter to Douglas on 8 September 1859, he returned to the subject:

The site selected by me for Government House is infinitely more worthy and affords ample facilities for all the attendant arrangements needful to such an Establishment. It is in juxtaposition to the Park,

4. Moody to Gosset, Attorney-General correspondence, 25 Aug. 1859.

5. Baynes to wife, Baynes correspondence, 6 Oct. 1859.

and will be surrounded by Public Reserve, while from its position it would be a commanding feature in a singularly beautiful natural combination.

It would be a peculiar gratification to me if your Excellency would sanction my making at least a commencement for a Building on a most moderate scale, and yet in some degree suitable as a Residence for a Governor of British Columbia.

The next spring, Moody sent drawings to Douglas of a design for Government House and drew a response in a friendlier vein:

. . . I have also received your note of the 20th June (1860) with the design of the House:

It is decidedly pretty and the arrangement comfortable. The two rooms on the upper floor will be required as bed rooms should I take any part of my family to New Westminster. In that case a bed room for my private Secretary will be wanted, and for that purpose a small building should be erected apart from the main building. In all other respects the design meets with my approval, and I beg you will have the building erected without delay.

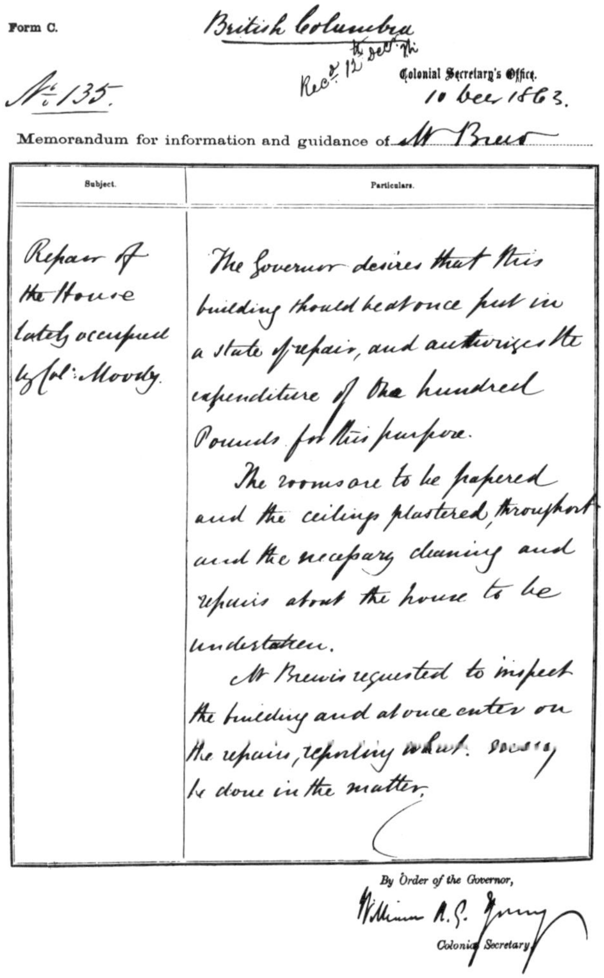

Form C.

British Columbia

Rec'd 12th Oct '63

Colonial Secretary's Office.

No. 135.

10 Oct 1863.

Memorandum for information and guidance of Mr Brew

Subject.	Particulars.
Repair of the House lately occupied by Col: Moody.	The Governor desires that this building should be at once put in a state of repair, and authorizes the expenditure of One hundred Pounds for this purpose. The rooms are to be papered and the ceilings plastered, throughout and the necessary cleaning and repairs about the house to be undertaken. Mr Brew is requested to inspect the building and at once enter on the repairs, reporting what [illegible] be done in the matter.

By Order of the Governor,

William A.G. Young

Colonial Secretary

Figure 11: Memo concerning Colonel Moody's house, 1863.

The drawings were made by John C. White, 2nd Corporal, R.E., who was to act as architect and oversee the work. The specifications were prepared and dated August 1860; but, on 30 July, Moody had already sent Douglas an abstract of tenders in which he recommended the low bid of 1253/8/0 pounds of Messrs. Graham and McLeese. He admits that "the sum named by your Excellency was one thousand Pounds" but adds, "That was previous to the additional accommodation" of the Secretary's quarters for which Douglas had asked. Douglas accepted the tender, the lowest of four—the highest being 1740 pounds.

On 16 August 1860, Captain R.M. Parsons of the Royal Engineers, writing for the Chief Commissioner of Lands and Works to the Colonial Secretary, asked Douglas to "move his Excellency the Governor to notify his sanction" for building materials for the house to be admitted duty free. Douglas refused and it then transpired (on 24 August) that Graham & McLeese, the contractors, had figured their tender on the assumption that duty would be waived as it had been for the buildings in the Engineers' Camp. The revised tender was 1343/8/0 pounds ($6,717 including $367 extra for lead flashing for valleys and chimneys). The letter from Parsons is endorsed by Douglas, in pencil, "Too late to finish the House this season and decline the terms now proposed". The contractors were so eager to do the job that they resubmitted a fresh tender at the original figure but were rebuffed again for the same reason.

By the end of May 1861, however, the sum of 3000 pounds had been allocated for the building. From a comparison of the plans and later photographs it seems that it was erected substantially as drawn, but the exact date of its completion is not known. It would seem that Moody moved into this house some time before he left the colony in November 1863. Chartres Brew, Acting Surveyor-

General in New Westminster, refers on 28 December 1863, to tenders for plastering, papering, and painting "the house lately occupied by Colonel Moody", in which several rooms require "Paper superior to what could be procured for 50 cents a Roll (and) the difference in price will have to be defrayed by Government." He notes also that "a good deal of cleaning will have to be done about the house and out-premises."

It was this structure in which Douglas took up temporary residence after Moody returned to England. Douglas arrived on 14 March 1864, eleven days before Arthur E. Kennedy landed in Victoria to replace him as Governor of Vancouver Island and stayed there almost until Frederick Seymour arrived in New Westminster to replace him as Governor of British Columbia on 20 April 1864. During this short period Douglas and his wife gave a fête at Government House on 31 March 1864 (six months after he had received his knighthood) which was his last public entertainment as Governor. His duty done, "Old Squaretoes" then retired to his own home in Victoria.

Because Douglas had resided in Victoria throughout his governorship of British Columbia he was constantly criticized by the mainland press for favouring Vancouver Island. In reaction, Seymour, the first Governor appointed exclusively for British Columbia, was most cordially welcomed. Seymour himself found the atmosphere of New Westminster highly congenial and when, in later years, it was proposed to move him to Victoria he wrote:

> In my own heart I must allow there was a feeling of favour of the manly, respectable, loyal and enterprising community established on the Banks of the Fraser.[6]

Seymour added a wing with a tower to the Government House. The additions were designed and supervised by architect J.C. White, who, as a corporal in the Royal Engineers, had designed the original house. His reward was 5 percent of the cost for his services, and the contract was for 865 pounds, with Angus H. Manson as contractor. In September, a separate cellar, probably used for roots, wine or ice, was built in the rear of the house. The cost was £46/7/10.

6. Seymour to Buckingham, Seymour despatches, 29 Apr. 1868.

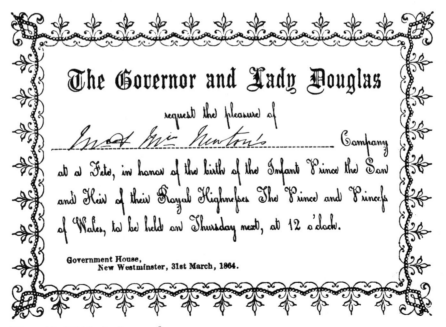

Figure 12: 1864 invitation to a fête.

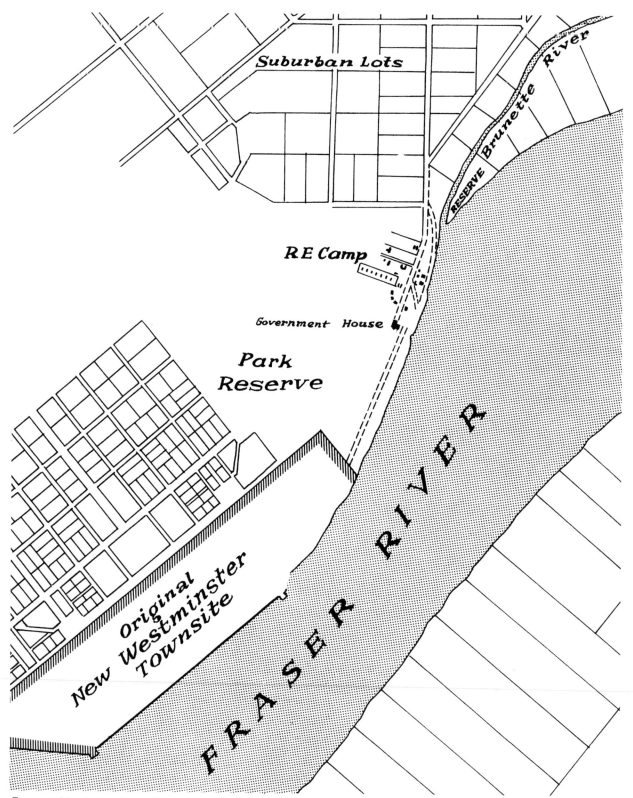

Figure 13: New Westminster, 1862. Original scale, 2 ?? to mile.

Evidently Seymour considered his accommodation barely adequate:

> I am at present in the occupation of Colonel Moody's house which I have made at the expense of the Colony, tolerably habitable, and which will obviate for a few years, if the Colony continues to languish, the necessity of building a new Government House... Colonel Moody laid out I am told 1000 pounds on this house

But to the colonists the house was Magnificence itself:

> ... The appearance of Government House, situated at the Royal Engineer Camp, about a mile from town, since it has been tenanted by Governor Seymour, has undergone a considerable change. Large additions have been made to the premises, including a magnificent lofty ball room, with large bow windows overlooking the lawn and the pretty river scenery. At the west end of the ball room... rises an ornamental tower which will much improve the appearance of the Vice-Regal residence from the river, when the shingles on the roof lose their new appearance and darken with age.[7]

The vice-regal residence quickly became the social centre of the burgeoning capital. On 8 November 1864, "The steamer Enterprise conveyed a number of guests (from Victoria) to the Royal Engineer Camp, and was conveniently moored at a landing immediately below Government House". Some 200 guests were received; dancing went on from 9:00 p.m. until midnight; then, "the doors of the supper room were thrown open disclosing one of the most elegant and tastefully arranged tables that we have seen at any private entertainment." Dancing was resumed until almost four o'clock in the morning when the band played the National Anthem and "many voices joined to do homage to England's Queen."[8]

The next major event in the Royal City's history was the Act of Union, proclaimed on 19 November 1866. Governor Seymour became the Governor of the new colony, and Kennedy resigned. One result of the union of Vancouver Island and British Columbia was the choice of New Westminster as the capital. The mainland was delighted, but New Westminster's jubilation was to be shortlived. In 1868, after two years of bitter feuding between the journalists of the two rival contenders for the capital, it was decided to move the capital of the united colony to Victoria. The announcement was made, cruelly, on the Queen's birthday – the traditional day of celebration in New Westminster. Seymour and his "court" moved to Victoria.

As an ironic recompense, New Westminster was later chosen as the site of the Lunatic Asylum and the Penitentiary. Both were built on the hill overlooking the erstwhile Government House and all three on land which had been Park Reserve.

Government House and grounds were now within the Penitentiary Reserve. The Dominion Department of Justice was responsible for the administration of the Penitentiary, but the work on all buildings and grounds was the responsibility of the Dominion Department of Public Works. There was considerable friction between the two Departments, and each year the *Reports of the Minister of Justice as to Penitentiaries in Canada* in the Dominion Sessional Papers (the only source of information, other than the newspapers, once the ownership was transferred) complained of the divided responsibility. For years the Penitentiary authorities tried in vain to get the use of Government House.

Two years after the Penitentiary Building was completed J.G. Moylan, Inspector of Penitentiaries, in his Annual Report 31 January 1880, complains:

> It is inconvenient and irregular for any person not connected officially with the institution to occupy any portion of the Penitentiary property. This is peculiarly the case in reference to the old Government House, which would answer as a suitable residence for the Warden, while the outlying buildings would furnish quarters for the married officers ... The objection which has been made to the surrender of this portion of the Reserve... on the score of its being required as a pic-nic ground for the citi-

7. *Colonist,* 11 Nov. 1864.
8. Ibid.

zens of New Westminster, should not... be entertained... There is no benevolence, no philanthropy in this pic-nic project. Were it entertained and advocated, with the full knowledge of the pangs and misery and envy, which the merry laugh, the gladsome shout, and the enjoyment... would excite in the breasts of their hapless fellow-beings nearby, it were not too much to say the proposition involves a strange desire of selfishness, nay heartlessness.

In January 1881, Moylan reports the old Government House "to be unoccupied, and the fine grounds surrounding it to be suffering injury from trespass" through being "thrown open for 'picnic parties'." But in the summer of that year the house was occupied by a Canadian Pacific Railway survey party under Mr. E. A. Wilmot, and in the following February they were enterprising enough to give the citizens a grand ball in the ballroom. "Notwithstanding the inclement state of the weather the number present was large and very brilliant. The ladies appeared to great advantage, the splendid old ballroom looking as well as it did in the heyday of the Seymour regime. Supper was laid in the centre room, the same which in General Moody's time was used as a sitting room, and nothing that could contribute to the comfort and enjoyment of the guests was wanting..."[9] The *Mainland Guardian* of 8 February added that "One of the engineers with an artistic turn, had executed some amusing sketches on the walls, which gave them quite [a] picturesque effect. The music – by our city band – was very good..." In May of the same year (1882), Lieutenant-Governor Trutch gave permission for the May Day celebrations to be held in the house and grounds.

On 2 July 1883, the Warden, Arthur H. McBride, (father of the later premier Sir Richard McBride), reports that Government House is still occupied by the Canadian Pacific Railway engineers.

> I have had the garden fenced off, as it was of no use to the engineers, and being left open, as it has been for the last eight or nine years, was only an attraction for stray cattle: many of the fine trees are nearly destroyed and all the handsome shrubs and choice plants have long since disappeared, although, since the Penitentiary was opened, I have done all that I could, under existing circumstances, to preserve the place.[10]

The year 1886 was an important year for New Westminster. The railway arrived. The ceremony of turning the first sod took place on 22 April at Sapperton. The penitentiary had now become a main reference point. The *British Columbian* of 1 May 1886, informs us that the mayor was advised of the Dominion Government's demand for a "nominal rent" in the sum of $50.00 per year to insure a 99 year right-of-way through the land lying in front of the penitentiary. The alterations were described. "The glen at Government House is being enclosed by a high wall, and that spot once so rich in natural beauty and so well adapted for pleasure grounds, will soon be shut out of view completely." Then the big maple tree, several hundred years old, near Government House was removed. Under it were found some Indian remains – "a rude coffin containing the bones of a child and...a dog". By July the track was laid along the river and the fence around the house removed. The press asked for the bridge (across the ravine) to be widened and the sidewalk extended, to tidy up an awkward job at small expense.

In August, Sir John A. Macdonald and his wife visited the western provinces. Lady Macdonald, evidently a woman of spirit, rode on the engine's cowcatcher through the Rockies so as not to miss any of the grandeur. The civic committee which arranged the reception of the Premier was given a rough time in the press about the casual arrangements and their parochial attitude in general. The party arrived after midnight and, in a torchlight procession, they went to the See House of Bishop A.W. Sillitoe. They spent the night there and at noon the next day were brought to Government House for lunch. (The City Council had been given permission to use it.) "The smallest room..., an ante chamber of the old ballroom, was selected for a parlour and there the lunch was laid; the cloth was

9. *British Columbian*, 8 Feb. 1882.

10. Cotton ms. does not give a source. Ed.

as white as snow, the roast beef and chicken excellent; there was a profusion of flowers and no
chairs..." Sir John was given credit for the railroad
and his reception by the people (who expected to
profit from the venture) was triumphant. It was a
field day with "markees and tents where cold
lunches, and cool drinks" were sold cheap to the
people by "enterprizing citizens."

Lady Macdonald, the local paper reported, "was
very much pleased with the old government house
grounds, and thought it a great pity the stately old
building had not been kept in better repair. In this
opinion we entirely concur."[11] The Inspector of
Penitentiaries also concurred; and indeed Moylan
had already given a graphic though possibly exag-
gerated description of its condition in his report of
25 November 1885:

> ... another objection, which I must take the liberty
> of characterising as puerile and absurd, has been
> offered. It has been sapiently set forth that, as this
> place had been once the residence of former Govern-
> ors of British Columbia, and as it commands a fine
> view of the Fraser, it would be a desecration—as it
> were—to convert it into quarters for a Warden of a
> Penitentiary! Rather ludicrous, particularly since
> the cows of the neighbourhood... enjoy the shelter
> of the hall and drawing rooms, from the fervid heat
> of summer and the cold blasts of winter. One of
> the large brick chimneys has fallen in through the
> roof and the *debris* covers the floor of one of the fine
> and spacious lower rooms. The whole building is fast
> going to ruin, and the grounds, which would have
> been tilled and kept in order, if handed over to the
> Penitentiary, as requested, are in wild disorder,
> overgrown with weeds and the walks and terraces
> trampled out of sight and form by the trespassing
> cattle..."

The next year Moylan recommends "once more,
that a residence be provided for the Warden on the
site of the old Government House," but it was not
until 1889 that this project was carried out. On July
2 McBride reports that "the contractors are nearly
finished with the cellar and general foundations."

According to his daughter, Miss Dorothea
McBride of New Westminster, "The original
House was torn down and the Warden's house
built on the same foundation".[12]

A comparison of the site plans of the two buildings corroborates her statement as to the site. It
would seem then that the grand old house, decayed
and disused, suffered the indignity of demolition
over the winter 1888-1889. Forty years later, on 7
February 1929, the Warden's house burned to the
ground and the *British Columbian* reported the loss
as being that of the original Government House. To
this day, many oldtimers in New Westminster
believe this fiction.

In closing the chapter of the New Westminster
Government House it is tempting to speculate, as
Seymour did, on what might have happened. In a
letter to the Duke of Buckingham, 2 February 1868,
he writes:

> The only building that has turned out to be of
> advantage to the Colony is the house Colonel
> Moody built for himself, but then it is inconvenient
> for people in the town to have to walk a mile when-
> ever they wish to see me. Had this house not existed
> it is probable that I should have built a larger and
> more commodious one in the city of New West-
> minster, out of the 10,000 pounds placed at my
> disposal for the purpose & then it is probable that
> the great expenditure incurred in Victoria in build-
> ing a Government House would not have arisen.[13]

11. *Mainland Guardian*, 18 Aug. and 24 July, 1886; *British Columbian*, 17 Aug. 1886.

12. D. McBride to Cummins, warden, 25 July 1957.
13. Seymour to Buckingham, Seymour despatches, 2 Feb. 1868.

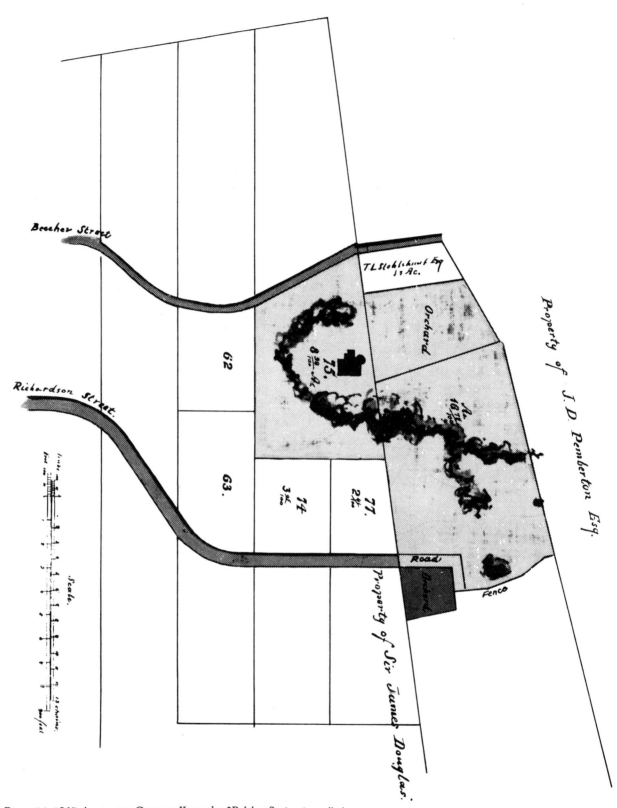

Figure 14: 1865 plan sent to Govenor Kennedy. *Belcher St. is mis-spelled.

CHAPTER THREE

Bleak House

WHEN CAPTAIN ARTHUR EDWARD KENNEDY arrived in Victoria on 25 March 1864, to succeed Douglas as Governor of Vancouver Island he was homeless. Douglas had lived in his own home, and Blanshard's house had been sold and moved. Initially Kennedy took up residence in the St. George's Hotel. By Christmas, the British government was finding the expense of its colonies a burden. The Duke of Newcastle, new Secretary of State for the Colonies, felt that it would be more economical to unite the colonies of British Columbia and Vancouver Island but, given the present mood of the colonists, it was unwise to insist. Instead of embarking on a policy leading to unification he decided to make each colony responsible for its own civil list. The House of Assembly of Vancouver Island was in no mood to use its dwindling funds for the "luxury" of a salary or residence for the Governor and said so. Kennedy's reception had cost the colonists some $2,000.00 and the Assembly refused to go beyond this.

The general public, however, had a different attitude, and meetings were held to agitate on Kennedy's behalf. Dr. J.S. Helmcken, in his reminiscences, tells of one of these at which he spoke against the expenditures:

> ... I was met with hisses and no end of uproar, so could say but little and felt very small—any one on the same side met with a similar fate and it was known afterwards that Gov. Kennedy and his Secretary Wakeford, were in one of the boxes with curtains closed. They must have been delighted, because it was hurled against me that I was only inebriated by jealousy and that the days of the Douglas regime had gone bye—never to be resumed —I was very foolish to have taken publicly any part in this housebuilding affair..."

When the news reached Nanaimo that the House

had refused to be more gracious and generous, a letter to the *Colonist,* signed by "Innuendo", warned that:

> you may expect to learn of the best house in Nanaimo being proffered His Excellency, or of the people building one... So if you don't 'look out' you may find the seat of Government transferred to Nanaimo before you are aware of the fact. Take warning from this.[1]

Before Kennedy arrived in Victoria, it had been said that Donald Fraser's house on Humboldt Street was being made ready for him. A second report indicated that, before he left London, Kennedy had had a London architect draw up plans for his Victoria residence to prevent delay. This was taken by the press as a slight to local talent.

> Intended to inculcate amongst us the taste for a higher order of architecture than our public buildings are said to exhibit. We might object to this part of the programme, on the ground that it discourages colonial enterprise; but the mere dread of obtaining another specimen Indiano–Dutch–Chinese order, as displayed in the pagoda wigwam across James Bay, at once reconciles us to the decision of the Duke.[2]

On 2 April, Kennedy informed the Legislative Assembly that he was willing to submit proposals for either a temporary or a permanent residence and enclosed as authority a letter from the Colonial Office stating:

> The duty of providing the Governor with adequate house accommodation devolves upon all Colonial

---

1. *Colonist,* 15 Apr. 1864.
2. *Colonist,* 5 Apr. 1864.

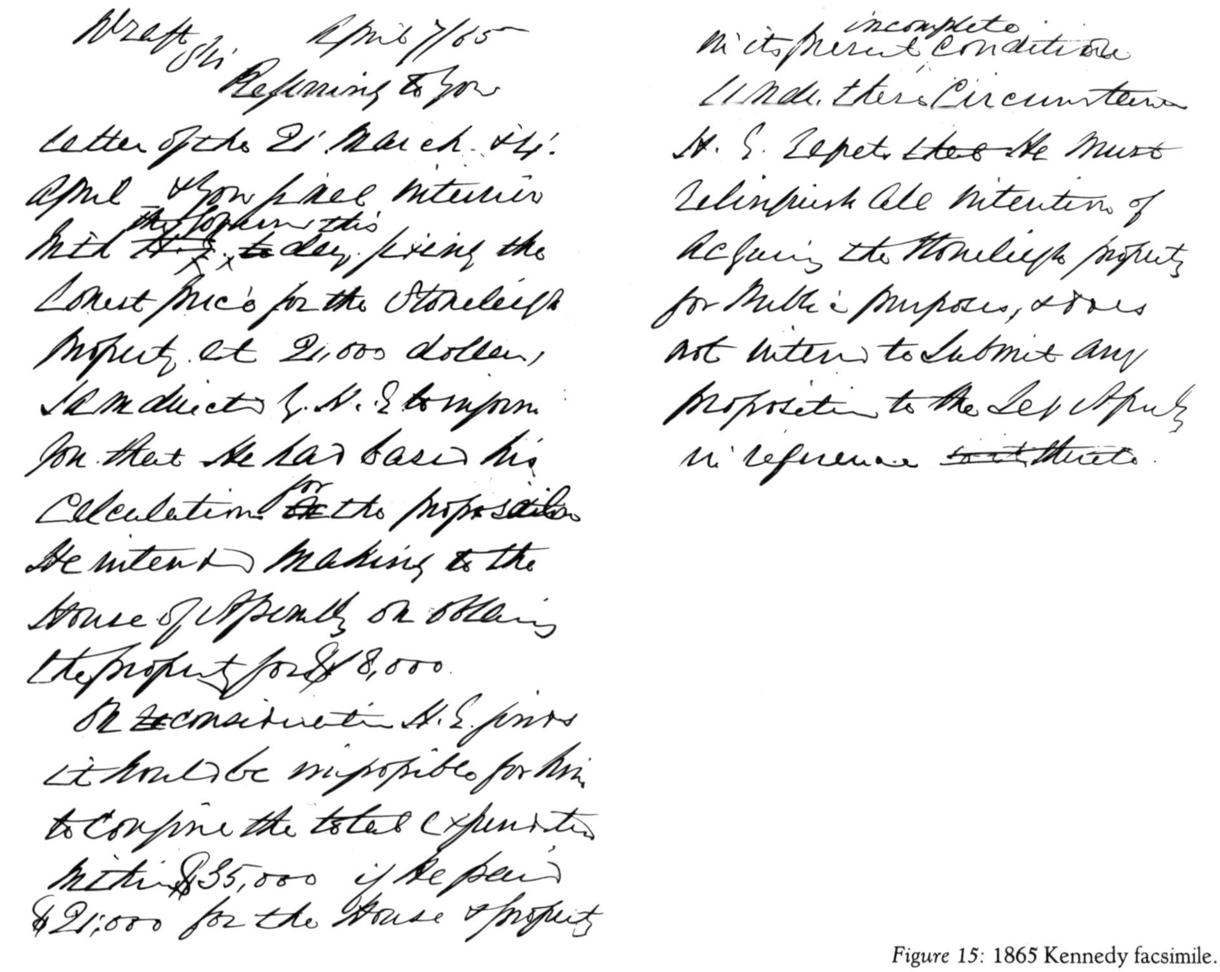

Draft Sir, April 7/65
Referring to your letter of the 21st March & 4th April & your personal interview with H.E. this day fixing the lowest price for the Stoneleigh property at 21,000 dollars, I am directed by H.E. to inform you that he had based his calculation for the proposition he intends making to the House of Assembly on obtaining the property for $18,000.
On consideration H.E. finds it would be impossible for him to confine the total expenditure within $35,000 if he paid $21,000 for the House & property in its present incomplete condition. Under these circumstances H.E. regrets that he must relinquish all intention of acquiring the Stoneleigh property for public purposes, & does not intend to submit any proposition to the Leg. Assembly in reference thereto.

Figure 15: 1865 Kennedy facsimile.

> Communities, and I entertain no doubt that the House of Assembly of Vancouver Island will cheerfully respond to your application.[3]

But these hopes were too sanguine. The House of Assembly—with no personal antipathy to the Governor—refused the expenditure. Kennedy then "temporarily secured the prettily situated residence of Mr. Jos. Trutch, the latter gentleman being about to proceed to England."[4] The Trutch house was probably quite adequate for himself, his wife and his daughters, but not large enough for the discharge of the social obligations of the Queen's representative. As such, he wrote:

> . . . My desire is to come into contact with all classes of the population, and I am only sorry that the house I have engaged will not afford me from its smallness, the opportunity of meeting as many of the inhabitants as I could wish.[5]

In the early spring of 1865, the House of Assembly re-opened the question of building a residence. It may seem strange that the Assembly would consider such an expense when a Government House occupied by Governor Seymour was already in existence in New Westminster and when arguments in favour of the union of the two colonies were being advanced. Kennedy had stated

3. Ibid.

4. Ibid.

5. *Colonist,* 13 Apr. 1864.

Home of Sir James and Lady Douglas, Victoria.

Royal Engineer Camp (now Sapperton), New Westminster, ca. 1860s, *photo:* F.G. Claudet.

Government House, New Westminster, ca. 1860s, *photo:* F.G. Claudet.

The Wardens Residence. Provincial Penitentiary. New Westminster B.C.

B.C. Penitentiary Warden's residence, New Westminster.

Trutch house, Victoria; Trutch family on lawn, ca. 1868.

Cary Castle, ca. 1860-65.

Cary Castle, ca. 1865-68.

Cary Castle, before 1870, *photo:* F. Dally.

Cary Castle from the southeast, ca. 1866-70, *photo:* F. Dally.

Cary Castle from the east; Cornwall family on lawn, 1881-87.

Eastern facade of Cary Castle, 1880s.

Cary Castle from the gates (view from the north-west).

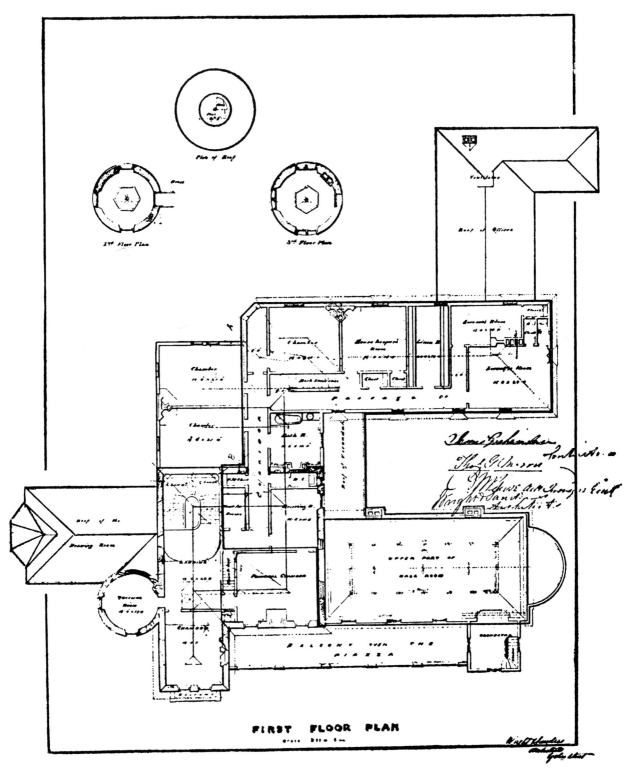

Figure 16: Proposed alterations to Cary Castle, 1865.

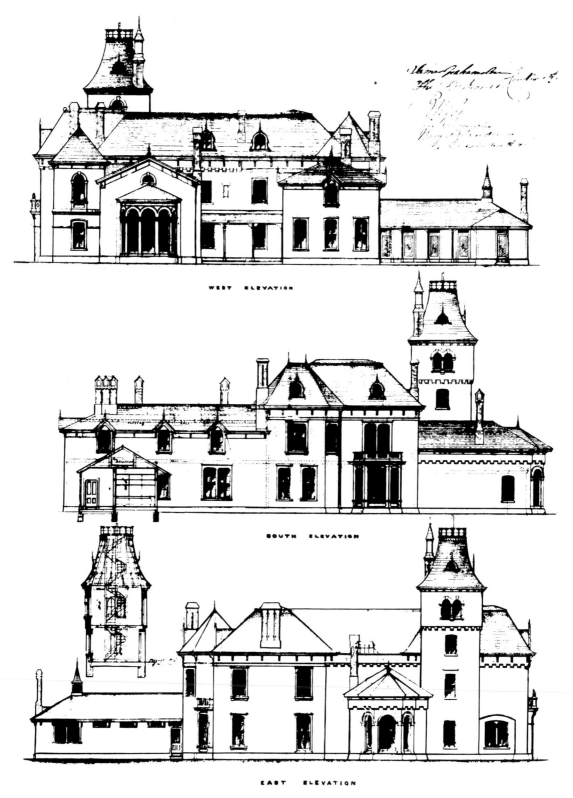

Figure 16: Continued.

publicly at a dinner that he had informed the Duke of Newcastle "he would willingly relinquish his appointment to this colony, if the Government thought fit to send Governor Seymour to rule over both colonies."[6] However, an editorial of 21 February 1865, noted that "if union took place to-morrow we should still be under the necessity of having the head of the Executive the principal portion of the time in Vancouver Island," and the editor argues further, "It is unjust...to have the Governor going about like a bird of passage, and paying rent like the most ordinary citizen in the place."[7]

When the House took up the question there was much discussion. To keep the costs down, it was suggested that some land owner might donate a site, "doubtless...on some of the great thorough-fares leading out of the city." Beacon Hill Park was not desirable, nor was there room on this (Parliament Buildings) Reserve or on any of the public squares. Dr. Helmcken jokingly suggested Ogden Point. Amor De Cosmos said the building "should be built of Newcastle stone...on a plan capable of being enlarged." A suggestion was even made to ask the Governor to send down estimates of the probable cost of what would suit him. De Cosmos thought this "rather a delicate matter", but Dr. Helmcken "could not see any want of delicacy... the House was becoming too sentimental." In the end the members voted $50,000 for site, building and furnishings.[8]

The same day, the *Colonist* editorial congratulated the House on its decision and took up the idea of a site being donated:

There is enough land lying idle and profitless around Victoria... and a grant... although evincing mag-naminity in the donor would not prove to him any very serious loss, a tasteful and substantial building ...will enhance considerably the value of the sur-rounding property. Independent of this there is some mysterious attraction in the vice-regal as well as regal dwelling that draws population in their immediate vicinity.

This admonishment had its effect. Captain William McNeill offered 10 acres on Foul Bay Road; The Hudson's Bay Company offered 25 acres on Esquimalt Road; Roderick Finlayson, 10 acres on Quadra and Queens; and J.D. Pemberton a choice of several "situations".

More than a month went by after the vote with no further reference to Government House. Then, suddenly:

An erroneous rumor is in circulation that Gover-nor Kennedy is about to purchase "Castle Cary" as the gubernatorial mansion. The Legislative Assem-bly voted the $50,000 to *build* a residence, and also indicated the material to be used, *viz.* the beautiful freestone found on the Island. The intention is to make the structure, both in material and architec-ture, an ornament to the colony.

Erroneous the report was not. Kennedy *had* bought Castle Cary.

It was presumed that he had "bought the prop-erty as a Personal investment, intending to use it as a temporary residence till the Government House contemplated by the Legislative Assembly is erec-ted, which cannot be done in less time than from 12 to 18 months".[10] Here lies, perhaps, one clue as to why he bought it. By October he was able to give a ball—in six months instead of eighteen. There was also the necessity of making a move out of the Trutch house since the owner and his family were expected back from England. They arrived in May of 1865. Kennedy's purchase of Cary Castle elimin-ated the necessity of spending time in an architec-tural competition as suggested by the *Colonist*:

So far as the building itself is concerned designs should at once be publicly tendered for. We cannot form any idea of the sketch or plan which His Excel-lency obtained in England. It may be a suitable one or it may not: but whatever it is we think, the public mind will only be satisfied by having the designing part of the work given out to public competition... When we obtain a design that will reflect credit

6. *Colonist*, 9 July 1864.
7. *Colonist*, 22 Feb. 1865.
8. Ibid.

9. *Colonist*, 1 Apr. 1865.
10. *Colonist*, 26 Apr. 1865.

upon the colony... and inculcate a higher taste for architecture amongst the inhabitants... the building material shall be island material and the best the colony can produce. With proper land management a respectable gubernatorial residence may be built and furnished for $50,000. It will not be a palace nor a building of very great pretentions, but it will on this account better suit the exigencies of the colony.[11]

There was no competition, although one firm of architects, Green & Oakley, saw the Governor and requested permission to prepare plans and estimates on the assumption that "any work required to be done in this matter professionally wd. be open to Public Competition, and... our Mr. Green was the architect of the original edifice."[12] But the Governor had already chosen Wright & Saunders to alter and add to the old building. B.W. Pearse, Acting Surveyor-General, advertised for prices from "Carpenters and Builders", whose tenders were to be "accompanied by the names of two persons... willing to become joint security for the undertaking, and completion of the contract within the specified time, in a sum equal to one-fourth the amount of the tender."[13] All this, despite questions in the house by De Cosmos, as to why a building was being purchased and not built.

This house which Kennedy had bought, and was now having altered, was called *Castle Cary* by the political opponents of its builder, George Hunter Cary. A lawyer, one of Lord Lytton's choices, he had been sent out as Attorney-General for British Columbia in 1859 and had soon become Attorney-General for Vancouver Island as well. He had a large private practice, so his earnings were considerable. Cary had bought some land from Douglas and J.D. Pemberton and, when he made money, Helmcken says, "he took it into his head to build a small castle of which he had a picture, but let him who buildeth a tower first count the cost thereof. The cost was very great—labour very high, so he

satisfied himself in the end with a wing...",[14] but in 1862 Cary "invested in the Never Sweat claim at Cariboo and other mining property and was soon financially ruined, and his fine residence... passed into the hands of the mortgagee."[15]

The mortgagee was Alexander Grant Dallas, Douglas' son-in-law. His $8,000 mortgage on Section 75 (due 1 January 1867, at 1½% interest per month) had to be paid off before Kennedy would accept the property. By this time, Dallas had retired to Scotland and his affairs were looked after by the same Donald Fraser who had bought Blanshard's house, and into whose house on Humboldt Street Kennedy was rumored to be moving when he arrived.

By September 1864, Elizabeth Miles, widow of the John Miles who had served as Clerk and accountant under Moody in 1859, was living in grandeur in Cary Castle. It would seem that she bought the house in December 1864. Mrs. Miles named the house *Stoneleigh* and gave its address as Belcher Road (a name since changed to the more euphonious Rockland Avenue). Its legal description was "Section 75 of Fairfield Estate, Victoria District, containing 8.98 acres, held under a lease forever from Sir James Douglas at a rental of 10 pounds Sterling per annum payable semi-annually, and comprising all that massive stone dwelling commonly known as 'Cary Castle' or 'Stoneleigh' further adjoining 16.78 acres, more or less, forming part of section LXVIII on the Official map of Victoria District". Curiously enough, £10 per annum was paid to Douglas and later to his estate until 1922, when a cash settlement of $1,000 extinguished his claim.

Cary had bought Section 75 from Douglas on 25 March 1851. The adjoining 16.78 acres he had bought from J.D. Pemberton in September 1859. This "Pemberton" property was acquired by Mrs. Miles on 15 March 1865. She herself says that it was she who "sold" Mrs. Kennedy on the idea of buying

---

11. *Colonist*, 22 Feb. 1865.

12. Green & Oakley to Kennedy, Green & Oakley correspondence, 27 Apr. 1865.

13. *Colonist*, 3 June 1865.

14. Helmcken, reminiscences, v. 4.

15. *Colonist*, 4 Mar. 1881.

all her Cary Castle property "at a less price than had been preivously asked," Sections 74 & 77 were offered as well (as leases), the transfers of which were made available for a premium of $500, with the privilege of purchase at 200 pounds an acre, at any time before the expiry date of 25 March 1883.[16] Both properties were rejected at the time, but became the property of the crown in 1909. A Mr. T.L. Stahlschmidt also owned one and a half acres on Belcher Road for which he asked $6,500 cash for the land and his dwelling (with the proviso that he continue to live there rent free until the end of 1865, thus allowing time to build another residence). Although this offer was also rejected, the property was subsequently acquired by the Government in 1877 for a sum of $3,500.

During the negotiations, Kennedy almost abandoned the whole project, for he was concerned that if he had to pay more than $18,000 for the property "in its present incomplete condition" there would not be enough left of the Legislative grant to alter and furnish the house.[17] Finally, however, on 3 June 1865, he took possession. The purchase price was $19,000 in U.S. Gold coin.

The original furnishings of Castle Cary had been assigned by Cary in a chattel mortgage for $1,500 to help defray the expenses on some cattle he had imported from San Francisco. He lost the furnishings and, incidentally, the cattle as well, in this transaction. Because of this and other financial reverses, he tendered his resignation as Attorney-General in August 1864. A brilliant and able lawyer, he gradually became more and more eccentric. He was arrested once for riding his horse at full gallop across the new James Bay bridge to the 'Birdcages' and another time he was clapped in jail to stop him from leaving for San Juan Island to fight a duel. Helmcken said of him, "He was all Lawyer and pleder [sic]—Genius and madness in him were closely allied." He returned to England in September 1865, and died insane a year later "of softening of the brain". Cary was one of the more colorful characters in the colony's early days and it is unfortunate that his only 'monument' in the colony he

enlivened has long since disappeared.

It began to disappear in the summer of 1865. The tenders which came in for the alterations and additions were all higher than anticipated, running from $21,000 to $24,000. While the Legislative Assembly had voted $50,000, Kennedy had volunteered to keep the total cost down to $35,000, thus saving the colony $15,000. To keep the cost of the work as low as possible, some of the proposed additions were deleted and the work done was of frame construction rather than of brick or stone. The stables contract went to John Toole and the well contract, originally, to William Baxter. Finally, however, the second well tender had to be accepted (at $19 a foot) since Baxter could not be found. The furniture contract went to Jeffreys Bros., "deserving mechanics of this city", and T.L. Fawcett got the contract for upholstery.

By the end of July, forty men, mostly plasterers, were working on the job. The roof of the original "castle" was not changed. The dining room, as well as the smoking room, verandah, balcony and orchestra, which were to have been connected with the ballroom, were postponed. Although the building would have been more handsome and prepossessing had the original plans been carried out, the *Colonist* noted that "Messrs. Grahamslaw & Morris . . . are making as good a building of it as the materials allow", and further declared:

> The plans, which are drawn up with the usual ability of Messrs. Wright & Sanders, look to an unprofessional eye very well indeed, and when carried out to the full design the erection must be admitted to present a creditable appearance. The round tower, carried a story higher and surmounted with a neat bell-shaped cupola and 'the flag that braved', etc. looks quite picturesque.[18]

Governor Kennedy was able to take possession in mid-July. The date of completion was to have been 1 October 1865, and a ball was scheduled shortly thereafter. However, some delay in the construction caused the ball to be postponed three weeks. It

16. *Colonist*, 13 July 1866.
17. Cotton ms. does not give a source. Ed.
18. *Daily Chronicle*, 31 July 1865.

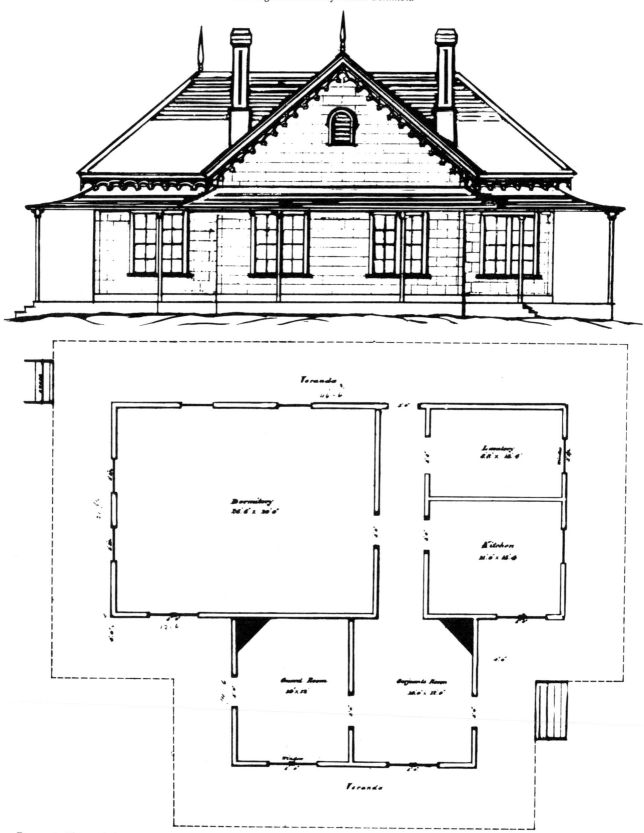

Figure 17: Plan and elevation of the Lodge, 1868.

was held on 26 October, and declared the largest, best and "most sociable affair ever to be held in the Colony." The *Daily Chronicle* reported on 28 October that "hitherto there have been few occasions, from want of a suitable building, in which the Governors of this Colony could bring together any large number of the colonists in the pleasing relation of honored guests of their chief ruler." The Sovereign's representative was now able to entertain his honored guests in a suitable setting:

> The ballroom, a fine loft and well ventilated apartment, 50 x 25 x 23 feet high, [has] a handsomely ornamented ceiling, from which were suspended three splendid chandeliers that diffused a brilliant light over the scene. On one side of the room are two elegant mantel pieces, one bearing the Colonial and the other the Royal Arms, which were much admired.

Some 400 persons attended and dancing continued until half-past three in the morning, "when the National Anthem was sung in chorus."

Two weeks later, the Ladies Committee of the Female Infirmary realized nearly $400 from an afternoon concert in the ballroom, and a second ball was held on 24 May 1866, at which "the programme was carried through with the greatest spirit" and a toast to the Governor "was drunk with unbounded enthusiasm".

The rest of 1866 was quiet socially although politically eventful. The colonies were still suffering from a depression, and the expenses of government were a burden heavy enough to make union of the two colonies seem more and more attractive. Apparently the Colonial Office in London was influenced by reports from Governor Seymour, who had returned to England, and the British government ended the separate existence of Vancouver Island by incorporating it with the mainland colony under the name British Columbia. The actual union was to take place on proclamation by the Governor. Which Governor? This question (and the question of where the capital was to be located) exercised the colonists far more than any long-range effects of the union.

When, for example, the newspaper reported that a telegram had been received requesting certain alterations to be made at Cary Castle it was agreed that orders had been given, but whether by Governor Kennedy or Governor Seymour was uncertain. "Is Victoria to be the capital, after all?" queried the *Colonist* on 28 September 1866. By October it was clear that Kennedy was being recalled and that Seymour would be the Governor of the united colonies. In October, it was publicly stated that the Kennedys would leave for home on the next steamer, and a committee was got together to prepare a farewell demonstration. A ball was decided upon, and permission sought from the Governor to use the Legislative Assembly. Tickets were sold, the band of the navy's flagship *Sutlej* was to play, and sailors were loaned for decorating the "ballroom".

On 18 October 1866, the afternoon before the ball, Kennedy had all his personal effects auctioned off at Government House, including a grand piano and two London carriages. The ball itself went off splendidly with the chandeliers of naval bayonets being specially remarked upon.

While Victoria was busy bidding farewell to Governor Kennedy the question of the capital was still unsettled. It was rumored that a petition was being circulated in the interior of British Columbia to have Lytton made the seat of the government. In Victoria the *Colonist* of 13 October 1866—the very day the Kennedys departed—quoted the *Cariboo Sentinel* of 11 October: "The next great bone of contention has been the seat of Government, and looking at the manner in which Governors have been treated in Victoria we should hesitate before confiding the Queen's representative to the tender mercies of the Victorians."

Before Governor Kennedy boarded the *Active* he swore in his Colonial Secretary, W.A.G. Young, as Administrator for the three weeks before "the Colony of Vancouver Island will have ended a brief but eventful career."[19] Coincidentally, the Kennedys' first home on the Island was also their last. From the day of the auction until they sailed, the Ken-

---

19. *Colonist*, 24 Oct. 1866.

nedy family stayed again at St. George's Hotel.

Governor Seymour and his bride arrived in Victoria from San Francisco on 7 November 1866. During the absence, his duties had been delegated to A.N. Birch, Administrator of British Columbia. When Seymour first landed in Victoria in 1864, the newspapers had observed that there were three governors in town, Kennedy, newly installed, Douglas, former Governor of British Columbia, and Seymour, Governor designate. This time Seymour was greeted by the Administrators of the two colonies which were awaiting his proclamation to unite them into one. The initial ceremonies on landing were brief, and he and his bride went at once to Government House. He later wrote to the Earl of Carnarvon:

> ...I was received with great coldness but no disrespect by a large concourse of people. I regretted to observe a look of extreme depression upon the Town and its inhabitants. As I would...take no share in the administration of the affairs of the Island until the union of the Colonies had been effected, I proceeded to New Westminster on the 10th Inst: to resume the duties of my office. I met with a most loyal and gratifying reception.[20]

The denizens of Victoria understood from local gossip that Seymour would leave his wife in Victoria while he made a quick trip to New Westminster. It is not known if she stayed or if she accompanied him but we do know his trip was not a quick one. Much to the consternation of the merchants, he was taken ill and the proclamation was delayed until 19 November 1866. Perhaps it is a coincidence or perhaps Seymour had a sense of history: the day he chose for his proclamation, 19 November, was the very day on which, in 1858, Douglas had proclaimed the existence of British Columbia. The official occasion was, by now, an anti-climax. Seymour reported:

> ...There was no enthusiasm or excitement shown in either town. Yet I believe that in each, the prevalent opinion is that a wise measure has been taken by the Imperial Government.[21]

Under the terms of union, New Westminster, the capital of British Columbia, was to be capital of the united colony. Seymour seems to have done his best to reconcile Victoria to this fact, adding in another letter:

> It may seem a trifling matter to mention, officially, but I would beg leave to state that during my month's stay in Victoria I gave three balls, which were very numberously attended. I do not believe that a single person invited declined to come for political reasons.[22]

The Governor was, however, more familiar with New Westminster than with Victoria, and personally he was far from displeased when the capital of the united colonies was fixed at the Royal City on the banks of the Fraser.

---

20. Seymour to Carnarvon, Seymour despatches, 20 Nov. 1866.
21. Seymour to Carnarvon, 21 Nov. 1866.

22. Seymour to Carnarvon, 11 Jan. 1867.

CHAPTER FOUR

Picturesque Old Pile

THE UNION OF BRITISH COLUMBIA AND VAN-
couver Island had now been effected and the
capital of British Columbia, New Westminster,
served as the seat of government for the colony.
During the eighteen months following the union
there was a most bitter strife between the capital
cities of the two original colonies. Governor Seymour tried to placate both parties by spending time
in each city; finally the choice was made on the
advice of the Legislative Council of British Columbia; the capital was fixed at Victoria.

Throughout the discussion Seymour maintained
an official neutrality. In mid-July 1867, he had
written resignedly to the Colonial Office: "Either
town will suit me equally well as a place of residence and in the present financial condition of the
Colony, I shall be very glad to have but one house
to keep up."[1] In truth, he found the expenses heavy,
for Seymour lived well, entertained generously, and
maintained what must have been the first private
steam yacht in this region. Yet his is but an echo of
Kennedy's earlier complaint: "A Government
House is now maintained here, but not at great
expense to the Colony—some of the expenses
which should properly be charged to the public are
now defrayed by the Governor."[2] Seymour, of
course, was in worse straits than Kennedy since he
had not one but two Government Houses. Six
months later he was still officially neutral when he
wrote: "Were either Victoria or New Westminster
prosperous it would matter but little where the
Governor had his abode."[3]

But in the same letter his personal preference is
clearly shown in his description of the two houses:

Victoria possesses . . . a Government House of some

pretentions built at a cost of about 9,000 pounds at
the time when the Colony could not meet its in-
debtedness. This house is large and unfurnished but
being situated amongst rocks so disposed as to keep
off the sun & not the cold breezes of the straits, it is
singularly unattractive. The walls have no paper to
hide the cracks which the settlement of the older
portions of the building have entailed upon them.
There is no water on the grounds in summer; all for
consumption has to be purchased.

Here however {i.e. New Westminster} the Government House is a cottage without pretentions on
the Banks of the Fraser. It is a modest English house
nicely furnished in a lovely situation and abun-
dantly supplied with water. I can hardly imagine a
Governor of his own free will leaving it for the more
ambitious building at Victoria which fails to supply
one of the necessaries of comfort after an outlay of
3 times as much as the House from which I now
write, has cost . . . .

Yet, although he would obviously have preferred to
live permanently in New Westminster, Governor
Seymour was genuinely concerned for the happi-
ness of the people of British Columbia. "If however", he continues, "we consider the question
merely as how to please immediately the greater
number of persons the selection of Victoria as Capital would be the most advisable." And when it
appeared from one of the Duke of Buckingham's despatches that Her Majesty's Government had
already arrived at the same conclusion, he declared:
"I propose allowing the inhabitants of both the
Rival Cities to eat their Xmas dinner in peace,
without letting them know that I have heard from
Your Grace on the subject."[4] It was not until 2 April
1868, that this despatch was laid before the Legis-

---

1. Seymour to Buckingham, Seymour despatches, 13 July 1867.
2. Kennedy to Cardwell, Kennedy despatches, 26 June 1866.
3. Seymour to Buckingham, Seymour despatches, 10 Dec. 1867.

4. Seymour to Buckingham, 13 Dec. 1867.

lative Council by the Governor. Acting upon their advice, he then made the final choice: Victoria was proclaimed the capital on Monday, 25 May 1868.

Now Seymour had to face the prospect of permanent instead of intermittent residence in Cary Castle. The alterations which Kennedy had sponsored in 1864, had been done as cheaply as possible and, as a result, within two years from its completion "the old building leaked so badly and had suffered so much in consequence that a considerable portion had to be pulled down and reconstructed to make it habitable."[5] Seymour tried to make the house comfortable as well; the improvements which he ordered at the time of Kennedy's withdrawal being described by the *Colonist* on 24 November 1866:

> The original Cary Castle is now scarcely recognizable; the old castellated roof has been removed, and a gothic roof, with dormer windows, substituted. The exterior stone-work has been slap-dashed or shingled [from 'shingle' in the sense of small beach stones], for protection from the weather, and various other improvements have been carried out by Mr. Grahamslaw, the contractor [one of the original contractors] in accordance with the original design [by Wright & Saunders. . . . The site of Government House is magnificent, and when the surrounding grounds are tastefully laid out and ornamented (which they, no doubt, soon will be), it will view with many of the more pretending [sic] gubernatorial mansions in older colonies.

Further minor changes were made by Seymour for "the two bronze chandeliers purchased at San Francisco in 1865 for the ballroom were replaced by cut glass ones from England".[6]

Nevertheless, in spite of repairs and reconstruction, Governor Seymour did not like the house. It was draughty, damp, and uncongenial to a governor who, in consequence of his residence in the West Indies, suffered recurrent bouts of dysentery. Moreover, his personal dislike of Cary Castle was no secret. The press had already commented on it:

If Dame Rumor is to be believed, Governor Seymour declines to inhabit Government House during his stay at Victoria, and has leased for the summer months the Admiral's residence at Esquimalt, which is to be immediately fitted up for the reception of the august party. The reasons given for selecting the Admiral's residences are that Government House is damp and requires extensive repairs, and that its situation is bleak, and consequently unsuited for the residence of persons in a delicate state of health. Thus had $50,000 been worse than squandered in the purchase of Cary Castle and the erection of the unsightly pile of buildings on the summit of a great rock in a locality exposed to every wind that blows.

Governor Kennedy never made a worse selection than when he took the advice of a professional friend and a notorious demagogue to buy Cary Castle first and consult the Assembly afterward. A more unsuitable location for a Government House could not well be imagined than the site of the Castle; but the Governor having declined to inhabit it, we hope that any extra expense to which he may be put by taking up his residence at Esquimalt will be defrayed from His Excellency's private purse.[7]

Seymour was spared this extra expense because the residence of Admiral George F. Hastings was not available, therefore, making the best of things, Seymour moved some furniture over from New Westminster house. He then tried to make Cary Castle more livable by adding a billiard room with a skylight, and new offices.

He also improved the grounds. In the spring of 1868, the Surveyor-General, B.W. Pearse, received orders from the Colonial Secretary:

> Proceed with the Croquet ground with all expedition, so that the dry weather does not overtake us before the turf is laid. (A serious problem – with all water having to be purchased at this time.) We can pay the cost from Crown Revenues. . . I want to get that little piece of garden under the drawing room window fenced in; and it would be very desirable to fence . . . the road up to the House . . . so as to prevent Cattle straying over the grounds.[8]

---

5. *Colonist*, 24 Nov. 1866.

6. D.C. Manusell to Seymour, memorandum, 21 Oct. 1867.

7. *Colonist*, 17 Apr. 1867.

8. W.A.G. Young to Pearse, Surveyor-General correspondence, 21 Mar. 1868.

In order to get the croquet ground done in a hurry, Pearse seems to have made use of the chain gang. This occasioned a great outcry in the *Colonist* of 10 April 1868, for, normally, the chain gang kept the streets of Victoria clean and its removal to Government House left piles of rubbish scattered around the city.

Time was now running out and the tone of the correspondence between Colonial Secretary and Surveyor-General became more and more agitated as the transfer of the Governor's official residence to Victoria became more imminent:

> Pray hurry on all you can. Never mind a few dollars. I will make that all square afterwards...I want the three upstairs rooms *papered*... also the Drawing room and the little round room... exercise your own taste for paper. For Drawing room white and gold. Little round room d[itt]o. For bedrooms something that is neat and pleasing to the eye — nothing gaudy or high colored. Pray rush on the work both inside and out with the utmost expedition.[9]

It was feared that the Governor might arrive from New Westminster before Cary Castle was ready for him; the Colonial Secretary wrote "in haste":

> ...The Governor had arranged to go down [to Victoria] on Wednesday. I have just been talking to Mrs. Seymour and have told her that he cannot go on Wednesday as the workmen will not be out of the house and the rooms up stairs will neither be dry or papered. She has promised me to get the Governor to postpone this moving.

The Governor's wife managed to delay her husband's arrival until 18 May.

Three months later a "barrack", which was really a guard house, was built on the grounds on Government House. The estimated cost of $2,000 was to come from Imperial funds. Admiral Hastings at Esquimalt was to provide a Sergeant and twelve men to mount the guard. The guard house was built substantially as drawn and the guard duly posted. Time must have hung heavily on the men's hands. Their consternation can be imagined when three days before Christmas the Chief Commissioner of Lands and Works, acting on the Governor's instructions, issued shovels, picks, grubbers, saws, axes, rakes, hoes, wheelbarrows and spades "for the use of the Governor's Guard."[10] Their employment in this respect no doubt saved the colony some money; but in other ways the Guard House added to the public expense of maintaining Cary Castle. The coal for Government House itself, the Guard House, and the house for propagating plants was paid for out of public funds with the Governor repaying only the cost of the coals consumed in his own private apartments.

The year after Seymour took up residence in Cary Castle the curiosity of Victoria was greatly excited by "three machines at the Express office directed to Governor Seymour". The public concluded that these were sewing machines, but, in fact, they were telegraph stands. It had been decided to connect the local telegraph office with the Colonial Secretary's office in James Bay and with Government House. Poles had already been brought from Burrard Inlet. Although the equipment addressed to the Governor was of a type which had been rejected as too slow by the American army during the Civil War, it was nevertheless expected that the machines would save His Excellency a considerable amount of time. The *Colonist* described him as "a first-class telegraphic operator" and this may well have been more than newspaper flattery.[11] Earlier, in 1865, when the Collins Overland Telegraph Company was commencing work at New Westminster on the British Columbia portion of its proposed line to the Bering Strait, Government House had been linked by wire with the city of New Westminster. Apparently, Seymour had been sufficiently interested to take lessons as an operator. According to the local paper "numerous messages were transmitted; but none, we regret to say, of a character suitable for publication."[12] Later, it was the Gover-

9. Young to Pearse, 8 May 1868.

10. Maunsell to Chief Commissioner, Lands and Works, Maunsell correspondence, 22 Dec. 1868.

11. Cotton ms. does not give the newspaper date. Ed.

12. *British Columbian*, 7 Mar. 1865.

nor himself who was at the wheel of his steam yacht *Leviathan* when, on 21 March 1865, the telegraphic cable under the Fraser was laid in seven minutes — the cable which carried as its first message between San Francisco and British Columbia, the news of President Lincoln's assassination.

Governor Seymour did not live to use the new telegraph in Cary Castle. By the time it was completed he was up the coast in H.M.S. *Sparrowhawk,* investigating trouble among the Indians. While there he suffered another attack of dysentery. He died at Bella Coola on 10 June 1869. His body was brought back to Victoria and after a state funeral was buried in the naval cemetery at Esquimalt.

Seymour's successor, Anthony Musgrave, then Governor of Newfoundland, was appointed immediately. However, until he could arrive in British Columbia, Philip J. Hankin, newly appointed Colonial Secretary and senior member of the Executive Council, became the administrator of the government. On 12 July 1869, Hankin reported to the Secretary of State for the Colonies, Lord Granville, that he had been unable to receive Admiral Cloue of the French frigate *L'Astree* at Government House because he had placed the House at the disposal of the late governor's widow. Mrs. Seymour left Victoria on 12 July; on 23 August, Governor Musgrave, a widower, arrived with his two sisters.

Since it was getting late in the season and he wanted to see the upper country before the following spring, Musgrave left Victoria on 7 September, for a tour of the Cariboo. He was enthusiastically received, with "demonstrations of Cordial Loyalty to the Queen, and of personal deference and consideration for myself as Her Majesty's Representative."[13] By the middle of October Musgrave was back in Victoria and, a fortnight later, suffered a severe fall when mounting his filly — an accident which resulted in a compound fracture of the leg from which he never completely recovered. On 27 December 1869, he wrote to Downing Street for a leave of absence the next April in order to visit New York on a personal matter. A month later he was still "Prisoner in my Bed". When April came he was obliged to tell Lord Granville that he had not

recovered sufficiently to take advantage of the permission and would prefer to go to San Francisco in June. The private matter, a secret well kept, was his marriage on 20 June 1870, to Jennie Lucinda Field, niece of Cyrus Field of Atlantic cable fame.

Only one ball seems to have been given at Government House during Musgrave's tenure of office. It took place on the Queen's Birthday in 1870, and was marred by a near tragedy: while the servants preparing for the ball were lighting the coal oil lamps, one of the six-lamp chandeliers crashed to the floor. The prompt use of blankets smothered the resulting blaze, but not before a portion of the floor had been charred and the walls blackened. Two hours later the room was filled with "ladies in light attire"; had the accident occurred then, "the effect would have been most serious".[14] This was a repetition on a larger scale of an accident in Governor Seymour's time when a coal oil lamp overturned and caused $800 damage. It was also but one of the many unheeded warnings pointing to the fate that was ultimately to destroy Cary Castle. Otherwise, the ball was a great success. To free as much of the floor for dancing as was possible, the band was put in a pavilion in the garden. The attendence was large and distinguished. H.M.S. *Boxer* brought, from San Juan Island, the commandant of the British Garrison, Captain W.A. Delacombe, and he and his wife, together with "Admirals Farquhar and Hornby, Capt. Hume and other Naval gentlemen [were] invited to remain at Government House through the holiday season."[15]

This entertainment and the wedding reception for the Governor's sister Zoe, who on 8 December 1870, married John Trutch, brother of Joseph Trutch (later to become the first Lieutenant-Governor of the Province of British Columbia), were the only major social events of Musgrave's incumbency. This may be accounted for partly by the Governor's continued ill-health after his fall and partly by the expense of maintaining the household at Cary Castle. Musgrave wrote to Lord Granville:

---

13. Musgrave to Granville, Musgrave despatches, 15 Oct. 1868.

14. *Colonist*, 26 May 1870.
15. *Colonist*, 24 May 1870.

Servants' wages are more than double the rates in Newfoundland or Halifax; there is some difficulty in procuring housemaids even at Fifty Pounds Sterling and their board; while almost all other prices and expenses are from fifty to one hundred per cent greater than in the Eastern Provinces, and I have not had the advantages of allowances such as that for light and fuel which was enjoyed at Newfoundland.[16]

Another possible reason for Musgrave's lack of lavish hospitality at Cary Castle may be found in the amount of time which he devoted to the problems of Confederation. He had been appointed by the Home Government to bring British Columbia into the Dominion of Canada and he had referred to himself in a letter to Downing Street on 2 September 1869, as "probably... the last Governor of the Colony." In another despatch he reported that a delegation of three was going to Ottawa to negotiate the terms of Confederation. One of the three British Columbians to go was Joseph William Trutch. The latter was going to England "on private affairs", at the conclusion of the talks in Ottawa, and would report further to the Colonial Office where, said Musgrave, he would "be able to afford Your Lordship any information which you may require in respect of the progress of the negotiations in which he will have been engaged. I place much confidence in Mr. Trutch's ability and discretion. Officials in London and Ottawa concurred with the Governor's opinion and indeed, so good an impression did Trutch make that, when Confederation was accomplished, he was selected by Sir John A. Macdonald as the first Lieutenant-Governor of British Columbia.

Trutch was in Ottawa when, in July 1871, he received his official appointment. Upon his arrival Lieutenant-Governor Trutch was to be enthusiastically received in British Columbia where he was already well known. A surveyor by profession, he had left England for California at the time of the gold rush, and had come to Victoria in 1859, succeeding Colonel Moody as Chief Commissioner of Lands and Works when the Royal Engineers left

the colony. It was Trutch's residence in Victoria, *Fairfield House*, rented by Governor Kennedy in 1864, which was now to serve, once more, as an official residence until the Lieutenant-Governor and his wife could move into Cary Castle.

Victoria had the good taste to give him a fitting reception and, having been widely entertained, Trutch returned the courtesy. On 9 November 1871, the Lieutenant-Governor, wearing what the newspaper called his "Civil Service uniform", received a large company of guests at a ball at Government House. The Trutches apparently were still living at Fairfield House as Cary Castle was badly in need of repair. Now that British Columbia had become a province of the Dominion of Canada, there was considerable confusion in the official mind as to who was responsible for the upkeep of Government House.

The estimates presented to the first Provincial Legislature in March 1872, included $5,500 for Government House, Victoria, but during the debate it became clear that the property was still owned by the Dominion Government, the transfer to the province having not yet been made. This raised an interesting question: if this property were offered, should the province accept it? If the province did not accept, Ottawa might turn Government House into a Marine Hospital or a Penitentiary—thereby depriving the province of a federal expenditure of some $30,000-$40,000 for the erection of new buildings for those purposes and leaving British Columbia to build an entirely new residence for the Lieutenant-Governor.

One member pointed out that Cary Castle had already cost some $100,000; that its market value was only $15,000, and that "woodpeckers and rats were destroying the plastered walls." Another insisted that the building would be "a dead loss to the colony as long as ever it stood" and suggested that only the roof be repaired at this time and that further repairs be deferred until it was certain where the Lieutenant-Governor would reside. Finally the sum of $2,000 for repairs was approved, together with another $1,500 for furniture, on the understanding that it would not be expended unless the Lieutenant-Governor actually went to

16. Musgrave to Granville, Musgrave despatches, 2 Sept. 1869.

live in Government House. No objection was raised to the expediture for water when it was pointed out that Governor Seymour had paid $65 a month for water delivered by cart and that workmen drilling for a well on Government House land had hit solid rock at forty feet. The house also approved expenditures of $350 for fuel and light; $200 for planting the grounds; $700 for the salary of the gardener and his assistants; and $250 for a new cedar fence enclosing the grounds. Also included in this year's estimates was $1250 for the Government House at New Westminster. When the need for two Government Houses was questioned, the Chief Commissioner of Lands and Works replied that "it was desirable to have the building kept in repair, and, in case the Government [sic] went up there for a short time, he would find a residence."[17]

No sooner were the estimates passed than "the noise of busy workmen was heard from the mouldering turrets... putting to flight the woodpeckers and rats." In a matter of weeks the "castle" was ready and the Lieutenant-Governor began his occupancy of "a palatial residence in one of the most paradisiacal spots to be found around Victoria."[18] Nevertheless, this sublime state of affairs was short-lived. In November 1872 the coachman's quarters in the Government House stables caught fire:

> His Excellency the Governor, with the servants of Government House, hastened to the spot... The chaingang were at work on the grounds, and, with their guards, also hastened to render assistance. Attempts were made to reach the roof, but the Ministry had failed to provide even a ladder... A messenger was despatched to town on horseback for the engines and the hooks and ladders, and the alarm being run by bells, the Fire Department and a large number of citizens were speedily moving towards the scene of conflagration. The Deluge engine arrived first... and, drawing water from a cistern... near the blazing stables, soon had two good streams playing on the fire.[19]

But to no avail: the building, which had been erected

in 1869 for Governor Musgrave at a cost of $4,000, was completely destroyed. No record of its rebuilding has been found but the stables were insured for $4,000 and, presumably, they were replaced immediately as the public accounts for 1873-74 show the sum of $43.75 for insurance on the Government House stables and $7 "for glue, etc., for repairs to stables."

Ever since Kennedy's time, the water supply of Government House had been a routine expense as well as a matter of continuous concern. The chronic water shortage made gardening on any large scale quite impossible, and fire was a constant threat. Surface wells had been dug, cisterns constructed, and shafts drilled but, finally, in 1876, the Government very sensibly decided that it would be cheaper to connect Government House with the Victoria City water system: "For an outlay less than one year's cost of carting water, Elk Lake water might be carried... to Government House through a 1½ or 2 inch pipe."[20] After endless bureaucratic delays this was done in 1887, the year before coal oil lamps were finally replaced by gas in Cary Castle.

By the spring of 1876, Joseph William Trutch's tenure of office was coming to an end and with it his popularity. As one of the negotiators of Confederation, he now had to bear the brunt of the public irritation which the Dominion Government had aroused by its delay in completing the transcontinental railway — the single most significant term of union. The enthusiasm with which his appointment had been received had dwindled to nothing:

> Has there been that cordial feeling between Governor and People that latter had a right to look for? What great, noble and patriotic cause has experienced the quickening influence of the gubernatorial smile? What public institution numbers our Governor amongst its list of patrons? Where have been the balls, the parties, and the "At Homes" that contributed so largely to public enjoyment and happiness in the past? True, the salary of the Lieut.-Governor is not so large as the salaries of his predecessors; but it is the same as those of the Lieut.-Governors in

17. For a full report of the debate see *Colonist*, 23 Mar. 1872.

18. *Colonist*, 15 Oct. 1872.

19. *Colonist*, 17 Nov. 1872.

20. *Colonist*, 2 Sept. 1876.

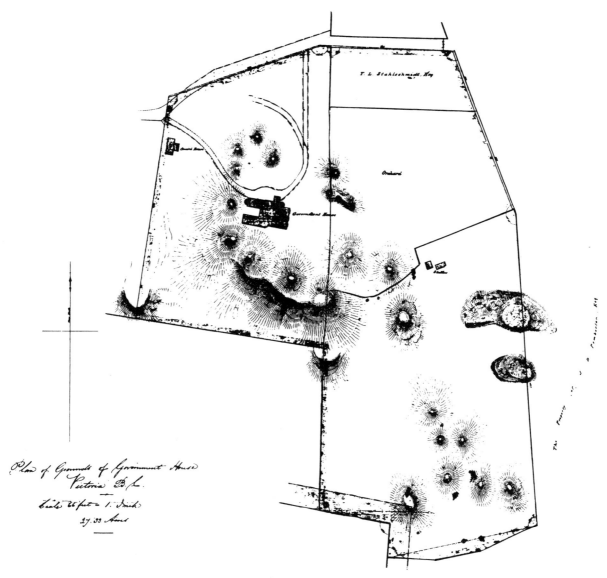

Figure 18: Cary Castle site plan; grounds in 1871.

other Provinces who do entertain the governed in a genuine spirit of hospitality.[21]

This attack upon a "home grown governor" brought a spirited defence from a local correspondent:

> . . . all his enemies can say is "He was selfish and he saved his wine." The insignificance of the accusation is an honor to the man. In a city where "uncharitable lines of society have been drawn" how could he

compliment Dick without offending Harry? Under such circumstances a man of feeling would do as he has done. He "saved his wine" and saved the people from the petty jealousies which are always springing up in the precincts of a petty court . . . Let him have a statue to his memory.[22]

In July 1876, Albert Norton Richards, Q.C., born in Ontario, was appointed to succeed Joseph William Trutch as Lieutenant-Governor. Richards had been active in Canadian politics. He had visited

---

21. *Colonist,* 23 May 1876.

22. Letter from "Punch" to *Colonist* editor, 27 May 1876.

British Columbia twice before settling in Victoria in 1873 and, in May 1876, he had been appointed legal advisor in British Columbia for the Dominion Government.

Thus, the new appointee (if not a "home-grown governor") at least had some experience in the province to recommend and help him. He was sworn in on 28 July 1876, but postponed moving into Government House because of the impending visit of the Governor-General, Lord Dufferin, who, with his wife, was to occupy the house during his stay in Victoria.

Years later, the Marchioness of Dufferin and Ava published the letters which she had written to her mother during her travels. She describes the local sentiment as being "British but anti-Canadian, on account of the railroad, which can't be made yet; so it is not all plain sailing." Indeed, the Governor-General spent a great deal of his time "shut up with various people," and she was left to amuse herself.

Victoria, 11th August, 1876.

The Lieutenant-Governor and Mrs. Richards

request the pleasure of the attendance of

in the grounds of Government House to take part in the reception which the Lieutenant-Governor understands is to be offered by the young ladies of Victoria to His Excellency the Governor-General and the Countess of Dufferin on the day of their arrival.

The Lieutenant-Governor regrets that the hospitalities of Government House cannot be offered on this occasion, as the house is reserved for the accommodation of the Governor-General and suite, and the Lieutenant-Governor and Mrs. Richards have to wait upon the Governor-General and the Countess of Dufferin at Esquimalt. Should the ladies have to stay any time at Government House, the ballroom will be placed at their disposal.

An answer is requested addressed to the Private Secretary, Government House.

Figure 19: 1876 Invitation.

Fortunately, she spent some time in writing and she describes the house and grounds of Cary Castle with the fresh eye of a stranger:

> This Government House is built on a rock, but a nice garden has been made; the drawback to it is the want of water. Every Drop, both for house and garden, has to be brought in barrels; so there is not much to spare, and the grass is all burnt up. From the windows there is a view of a magnificent range of mountains, a little wanting in variety of outline, but extremely high... Between us and them there is the sea....
>
> The house is very nice and comfortable: there is a good ball-room, small drawing-room, large billiard room, and excellent bedrooms. We have a Chinese cook who is, I grieve to say, highly British, having cooked for six Governors, but he is very good in his homely style; Ah Sam is his name. Then I have a very comfortable sort of housekeeper, a housemaid with a Chinaman under her, our own four servants, and a coachman and a gardener...

Thursday, the day after the Dufferins arrived, they "called on the Lieutenant-Governor—Mr. Richards, and drove round the city." Friday they gave a dinner for the Richards. Saturday they had a "Drawing Room" at the Parliament Buildings; Monday afternoon Lady Dufferin was "At Home", and in the evening they gave another dinner. Tuesday afternoon they had a garden-party and dance; in the evening they "had afterwards to attend a concert held in the theatre". Wednesday they attended a regatta at the Gorge, and in the evening there was a dinner party from which "we were obliged to dismiss our guests rather early, as we embarked after they left."

The Dufferins' trip took them up the coast to the Alaska border and back; then through New Westminster to Kamloops. They did not stop at Government House in New Westminster but returned to Victoria on 14 September 1876, in a heavy rain which "only made our drawing-room, with its fire and lights, look more than ever comfortable after all our travelling..."

The next morning Lady Dufferin had a surprise.

> Fred Ward, who is "housekeeper", has ordered up the prisoners from the Penitentiary to "pluck chick-

ens" for the ball; it is the custom here, and this morning, when we walked into the ball-room, we found six prisoners, with chains to their legs and an armed man standing over them, polishing the floor...

...Fred brought the head gardener into the drawing-room to give him some directions about flowers, and was about to take him to the dining-room, when he said, "I can't leave that man here; he's a convict." When the ball that evening started, Lady Dufferin was somewhat apprehensive. There was a rumour that the great Ah Sam was drunk, and that the supper would be very bad; but the dinner was all right, so we felt some hope... Soon after nine D. and I came down to open the ball. The room is a very nice one, and we had had all the windows taken out, and a sort of corridor tent of canvas, lined with flags, put up the whole way round the outside, which added greatly to the available space. I must say I enjoyed the ball very much, and I think everyone else did. We all danced from 9:30 till three without intermission, and as fathers, mothers, daughters and sons are all equally dancing-mad here, and as we had a great number of naval officers, and were in ourselves an element of novelty to the Victorians, and they were new to us, there was a great deal of spirit in the ball. When everyone else had gone, we had some more supper and a talk; the former was very good, and Ah Sam had been maligned.

The next day "we breakfasted at eleven, and had to start immediately after for the Esquimalt Dockyard... D. was to drive in the first pile of a new dry dock." The day after that, one of their duties took them "off to the Cathedral to attend the christening of a baby—'Frederick Temple Cornwall'".[23] This baby was the son of Senator Clement Cornwall whose home near Ashcroft the Dufferins had visited on their trip to Kamloops. The following day, 21 September, they left for San Francisco after the greatest social whirl Victoria had ever experienced. Four days later the Richards took up residence.

Like so many other governors, Richards started off his career with the good will and high hopes of the citizens being conveyed in innumerable addres-ses. It was his reply to one of these addresses on which his popularity foundered. It was the same issue that had cost Trutch the public's confidence: the railway. In an answer to an address from "the citizens of Yale"—five of them anyway—Richards expressed his gratification "to hear that you do not sympathize with the view that separation {from Canada} must result from the non-commencement of railway" which expressed his belief that few other sympathizers with separation existed.[24] An innocent enough remark in itself, it was spark to the tinder of resentment in the citizens of Victoria, who were distressed that the "Carnarvon terms" were being "dishonored". Level heads tried to reduce the incident to a reasonable perspective but a scapegoat was needed and Richards was it. "Though regulated by an unwritten code the limits of a Governor's tether are well ascertained" even if he "keeps his rope at its tightest stretch."[25]

By 9 November, members of The Carnarvon Club (whom Premier Elliot called constituents, although admitting them to be a "secret political organization") were out for blood, and suggested that if Richards could not be made to realize his proper limitations his "supplies" should be cut off. Elliott was, apparently, taken aback, but, while acknowledging that his ministry was annoyed, he pointed out that Ottawa, not he, controlled the Lieutenant-Governor's salary. The deputation, "not to be out-generalled", then suggested that the Legislature stop the salary of the Private Secretary or cut off the water and fuel allowance. Elliott "did not rudely dispel the pleasant conviction" that his Honour could be intimidated. Month by month the incident rankled. Richards' "amiable indiscretion" provoked "language...toward His Honour that no conceivable conduct of his would have justified." The pressure mounted to oust Richards by any means, "even, in case of need, the unroofing of Government House."[26]

During the uproar, Richards maintained a digni-

23. All quotations concerning the Dufferins are from Marchion-of Dufferin and Ava, *My Canadian Journal 1872-8*, 1891.

24. *Colonist*, 26 Oct. 1876.
25. *Colonist*, 24 Oct. 1876.
26. Quotations in this paragraph are from the *Colonist*, 9 Nov. and 12 Dec. 1876.

fied silence. "For diverse causes and considerations, and taking into consideration the ease and convenience of Our loving subjects" the meeting of parliament was postponed five times until 21 February 1877.[27] The press were so eager to get a copy of the estimates that, by dubious means, they obtained them before they were tabled in the House. They must have been disappointed to find all the usual sums for Government House still included.

Evidently Richards was not disappointed: a week after prorogation, 300 guests attended theatricals and a ball at Government House. The play was "Blow for Blow" by Henry J. Byron, and the extempore stage is well described: "The ball-room was divided off and a stage erected at the west end making a perfect little *bijou* of a theatre."[28] During supper the seats were removed and dancing followed.

There was something sadly ironic and prophetic about that play for, in the summer of 1878, when the House met again (after innumerable delays to consider estimates) the axe fell. Although $1750 had been allocated Government House by the Elliott administration for the first six months of the year, the new government now provided only $324 for the remainder of the year—a paltry $150 for building repairs, $150 for furniture repairs and nothing for water, fuel and light. Admittedly, money was tight and other votes suffered as well. An overall entrenchment from the "rash and lavish expenditure" of the Elliott Government was under way but Premier Walkem was almost smug in reporting that "the expenses of Government House had been reduced about $2000."[29] The reduction found general acceptance for there was little debate in the Legislature, and it went almost unremarked in the press. Its impact was felt immediately: one of His Honour's private secretaries had to be dismissed even before the estimates were finally approved.

Richards acted quickly by giving notice to his servants, and it was rumoured that he would rent a residence in town and surrender Government House "to the bats and owls." Well might the rumor fly. Richards was now thoroughly aroused by the situation, and on 22 August, he wrote a confidential despatch to the Secretary of State in Ottawa pointing out that "if the local authorities persist in enforcing the several reductions, he (the Lieutenant-Governor) will be obliged to vacate the Government House and live as a private Gentleman in a smaller house giving up the usual entertainments dispensed by persons in his position." He hoped the Dominion Government would not object to this proposal and would communicate their views to him "as soon as possible."[30]

Ottawa was sufficiently concerned to refer this despatch to a committee of the Privy Council and, in due course, on 2 October, over the signature of the Prime Minister, Alexander Mackenzie, a report was made:

> The Dominion Government only provide the salaries of Lieutenant Governors of Provinces, leaving it to the respective local Legislatures and Governments to provide such other services as may be necessary to ensure a proper discharge of the high duties of the office both in respect of the actual indispensable work connected with the Government and the hospitalities which seem to be an actual necessity of the position.
>
> Hitherto all the local Governments have shown that they appreciated the necessity of making reasonable provisions for the maintenance of the Government House—British Columbia being the most economical of all. The Dominion Government have, however, no means of enforcing any regulation respecting such expenditures.
>
> It is not absolutely indispensable that a Lieut. Governor should give a series of Entertainments, but it has always been the practice for Governors, whether appointed by the Imperial or Dominion Governments, to receive distinguished Strangers and Naval and Military Officers at Government House, and also to receive ordinary Citizens and public men of the Province, and it would be a matter of regret if in any of the Provinces local arrangements resulted in the suspension of such customs.

---

27. Legislative Assembly, *Journals*, 1877.

28. *Colonist*, 27 Apr. 1877.

29. *Daily Standard*, 27 AUG. 1878.

30. The original despatch is not available, but its contents are summarized in the Report of a Committee of the Privy Council cited in the following note.

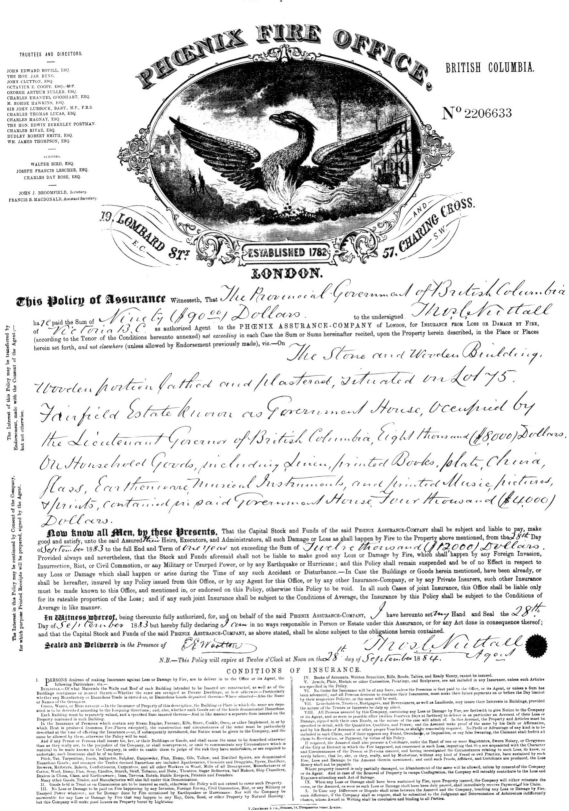

PHŒNIX FIRE OFFICE.

BRITISH COLUMBIA.

Nº 2206633

19, LOMBARD ST. E.C. — AND — 57, CHARING CROSS. S.W.

ESTABLISHED 1782

LONDON.

This Policy of Assurance Witnesseth, That *The Provincial Government of British Columbia* ha *ve* paid the Sum of *Ninety ($90.00) Dollars.* to the undersigned *Thos. L. Nuttall* of *Victoria B.C.* as authorized Agent to the PHŒNIX ASSURANCE-COMPANY of LONDON, for Insurance FROM LOSS OR DAMAGE BY FIRE, (according to the Tenor of the Conditions hereunto annexed) *not exceeding* in each Case the Sum or Sums hereinafter recited, upon the Property herein described, in the Place or Places herein set forth, *and not elsewhere* (unless allowed by Endorsement previously made), viz.—On *The Stone and Wooden Building, Wooden portion lathed and plastered, Situated on Lot 75. Fairfield Estate known as Government House, Occupied by the Lieutenant Governor of British Columbia, Eight thousand ($8000) Dollars. On Household Goods, including Linen, printed Books, plate, China, Glass, Earthenware, Musical Instruments, and printed Music, pictures, & prints, contained in said Government House, Four thousand ($4000) Dollars.*

Now know all Men, by these Presents, That the Capital Stock and Funds of the said PHŒNIX ASSURANCE-COMPANY shall be subject and liable to pay, make good and satisfy, unto the said Assured *their* Heirs, Executors, and Administrators, all such Damage or Loss as shall happen by Fire to the Property above mentioned, from the *28th* Day of *September 1883* to the full End and Term of *One year* not exceeding the Sum of *Twelve thousand ($12000) Dollars.* Provided always and nevertheless, that the Stock and Funds aforesaid shall not be liable to make good any Loss or Damage by Fire, which shall happen by any Foreign Invasion, Insurrection, Riot, or Civil Commotion, or any Military or Usurped Power, or by any Earthquake or Hurricane ; and this Policy shall remain suspended and be of no Effect in respect to any Loss or Damage which shall happen or arise during the Time of any such Accident or Disturbance.—In Case the Buildings or Goods herein mentioned, have been already, or shall be hereafter, insured by any Policy issued from this Office, or by any Agent for this Office, or by any other Insurance-Company, or by any Private Insurers, such other Insurance must be made known to this Office, and mentioned in, or endorsed on this Policy, otherwise this Policy to be void. In all such Cases of joint Insurance, this Office shall be liable only for its rateable proportion of the Loss ; and if any such joint Insurance shall be subject to the Conditions of Average, the Insurance by this Policy shall be subject to the Conditions of Average in like manner.

In Witness whereof, being thereunto fully authorized, for, and on behalf of the said PHŒNIX ASSURANCE-COMPANY, *I* have hereunto set *my* Hand and Seal the *28th* Day of *September 1883* but hereby fully declaring *I am* in no ways responsible in Person or Estate under this Assurance, or for any Act done in consequence thereof ; and that the Capital Stock and Funds of the said PHŒNIX ASSURANCE-COMPANY, as above stated, shall be alone subject to the obligations herein contained.

Sealed and Delivered in the Presence of *E. E. Wootton* *Thos. L. Nuttall Agent*

N.B.—This Policy will expire at Twelve o'Clock at Noon on the *28* day of *September* 18 *84.*

CONDITIONS OF INSURANCE.

Figure 20: 1883 Fire Insurance Policy.

The undersigned recommends that His Honor the Lieutenant Governor be informed that the Dominion Government will interpose no objection to his carrying out his views if he finds it absolutely necessary to do so, and also that the Government of British Columbia should be asked to endeavour to avoid the necessity of adopting what must be regarded as an unfortunate if not an unseemly course affecting the position of the highest personage in the Province.[31]

Lieutenant-Governor Richards promptly forwarded this report to his responsible ministers, but they were not to be diverted from their "unfortunate if not... unseemly course" for, again in 1879 and 1880, no allowance for fuel, light and water was voted.

The provincial government, however, could not shirk its responsibility for repairs to Government House. During the winter of 1878-79, if $1600 had not been spent, it is probable that irreparable damage would have resulted. The Chief Commissioner of Lands and Works thus describes the crisis he met:

> During the October rains, this building commenced to leak so badly that considerable loss seemed inevitable from impending destruction to the ceilings, walls, and furniture of some of the principal apartments, into which the water freely flowed from defects in the roof.[32]

A "mechanic" sent to examine the building estimated that from $250 to $400 should cover the cost of the repairs. They were immediately ordered. Between showers, enough roof was stripped to disclose damage much worse than anticipated.

> Shingles apparently sound were found to be split or rotten, entailing the necessity of re-shingling the entire roof. The gutters were... full of holes and cracks, as well as out of grade,—defects which caused the water to run down the sides of the build-

ing, destroying the outside plastering, and make the walls on the inside of the House wet. The timbers supporting the valley gutters proved to be badly strained and decayed, and the principal part of the tinwork utterly worn out.

To stop the work in such weather or to postpone it was impossible, for it would only have increased the damage and the ultimate cost of repairs. The urgency of the situation precluded the calling of tenders, for the job was done to prevent more "mischief by daily decay".

Walkem's review of the history of the decay at Government House makes a melancholy reading:

> From the outset the building has been a continual source of heavy expense. This may be partly accounted for by the composite form of the structure—part wood, part stone, the one settling deeper than the other in some places, and more rapidly in others; and partly from the nature of the foundations of the wooden portion, some of the sills of which rest on piers placed on rock, while others are laid on clay. These irregularities in the foundations cause the building to settle unevenly, and thereby damage the gutters and crack the plaster and ceilings. The building is also too low, or, in other words, the floors are too close to the ground, which gives very imperfect ventilation, and causes injury to the sills, joists, and flooring. The house and furniture are insured for the sum of $31,000, which is much below the estimated value of the property.[33]

Even the "bats and owls" would have found the house dreary, and Richards had certainly chosen an opportune time to threaten to remove himself from Government House. It is uncertain, however, whether or not he ever did so. He was living a quiet and obscure life as the only entertainment recorded between April 1877, and his retirement, occurred in March 1879, when his wife invited the Principal, teachers and pupils of Angela College, where her daughter was enrolled, to pass "a very pleasant afternoon" at Government House.

Richards' life at Government House was attended by many petty annoyances—deliberate or

---

31. Copy of Report of a Committee of the Privy Council, in Secretary of State to Lieutenant-Governor, Lieutenant-Governor's papers, 2 Oct. 1878.

32. *Sessional Papers,* 1879. Premier George Anthony Walkem (1878-82) was also Chief Commissioner of Lands and Works.

33. Ibid.

not—about which he complained, always correctly, through his Private Secretary to his ministers. Would they please remove the plate, linen, and pictures bought for the visit of Governor-General Dufferin? Would they please provide a new flag and halyards as "there has been only a torn Flag since His Honour has resided here?" The coal was of poor quality—no heat and impossible to burn— could he order a different brand? The messenger needed his salary raised from $25 a month to $30 as he found it impossible "to buy proper black clothes such as servants at Government House ought to have." The grate in his office had fallen out while the fire was alight; would they take steps to prevent its reocurrence as the consequences might be serious." Would they send the chain gang up Monday and Thursday to tidy up the grounds, water the gardens, mend the fences, and pump water—this last request most pressing of all "on account of the chain-gang not having come up to pump water here for so long that the water-closets are entirely without water and that the smell is going all through the house."

The lack of color and brilliance that characterized Richards' residence at Government House drew, some months after his retirement, a shrewd editorial from the *Colonist.*

> When Lieut.-Governor Richards first took office he entertained to a certain extent, or rather an uncertain extent, and showed some civility to distinguished visitors arriving in the province, but during the past three years of his incumbency Government House was virtually closed to those who were accustomed to participate in its hospitalities. Nor did the evil end there. Not only was the expenditure properly attached to Government House lost to the province but the expenditure of those who used to attend its entertainments—for every dollar spent at Government House ten at least would be spent by the guests in various ways, such as dress, gloves, millinery, and carriage hire, so that if the governor spent $900, the people would spend $9,000. This will convey some idea of the loss to the country, and all to save a paltry $700 or $800 formerly allowed the governor for fuel, water, etc., and what is this niggardly saving for? Perchance to be wasted on some unremunerative folly or in a wharf on the mighty Fraser. Mr. Richards had the reputation of not being overfond of entertaining; be that as it may, it is very clear that the mean parsimony of the government gave him opportunity to indulge in saving propensities. They cut off the supplies... and he closed the doors virtually. Through the neglect and decay of Government House our present governor has to live in a hired house at an inconvenient distance from the capital... Government House instead of being what it is in other parts of the world—the center of society—an attraction and a stimulating element in our midst, cheering young and old with suitable entertainments and kindly, notice, it is now a howling wilderness, a veritable blank. Let the Assembly no longer furnish an excuse for such a condition of things.[34]

The government now seemed prepared to modify its position; perhaps because its finances were improving and, perhaps also, because there was a new Lieutenant-Governor. English by birth and a lawyer by profession, Clement Francis Cornwall had come to British Columbia in 1862, with his brother Henry, at the time of the Cariboo gold rush. They never reached the mines; instead they pre-empted land which became the nucleus of their well-known ranch and its road house, Ashcroft Manor. Clement Cornwall had served in the colonial legislatures and had been appointed one of the three original Senators in 1871, which office he resigned to accept appointment as Lieutenant-Governor in June 1881. He was sworn in at a "large and brilliant" assembly on 20 July 1881—the tenth anniversary of the union with Canada.

Presumably, by the end of the year the Cornwalls were in residence at Government House where, judging from the report of Walkem, extensive alterations and repairs had been effected:

> The ceilings and walls of several of the rooms at Government House have been repaired, kalsomined, and colour-washed, and the floors, windows, roof, and outside walls of the building, have been put in good order. Carpets have been taken up, cleaned and relaid, broken furniture repaired, and the household effects generally well cared for. The tanks and cisterns have been thoroughly cleaned, and their

34. *Colonist,* 15 Dec. 1881.

filter beds relaid with fresh charcoal and gravel. The lodge, green-house, stables, drains, and fences, in and about the grounds, have been substantially repaired.[35]

Inventories, in rough draft form, exist of the furnishings of the House at this period. They give a flavour of the time and of official taste. The front hall had four stained benches, one stained table, one marble-top table and two pairs of antlers. Among other items – in other rooms – are strange things like "black rugs (imitation bear skins)", "programme register" in the ball room, and "Moderator (China) lamp". An extension oak table with 18 carved oak chairs (in green plush) and four pictures of the Royal Family were in the dining room. One office desk (carved oak), telephone and battery, copying press and stand, inkstand and album were among the furnishings of His Honour's office. The typical bedroom was furnished with an iron bedstead, spring, mattress, and paillasse, bolster, pillows, three pairs of blankets, marble-top table, mirror, chamber set, slop bucket, hip bath, coal scuttle and fire irons, rep curtains, blinds, chintz-covered furniture, and a wardrobe. Carpet, over oilcloth, was on the floor. The Royal bedroom had a "canopy brass double bedstead" with feather bed, a pier glass and chintz curtains to raise its standard above that of the others.

This was the house described by Princess Louise as "halfway between heaven and Balmoral," when, in 1882, she accompanied her husband, the Marquis of Lorne, on his first official visit to British Columbia as Governor-General.[36] The vice-regal party arrived on 19 September, and remained on board H.M.S. Comus that evening. The next day they moved to Cary Castle where, "a royal standard for the first time floated proudly over Government House". The party stayed until 7 December, and, while her husband visited various parts of the province, Her Royal Highness occupied the Castle. During this time, His Honour and Mrs. Cornwall lived at Maplehurst, a large house on Blanshard Street at Pembroke built in the 1860's, for Henry

Rhodes. The rent was $200 a month. In 1885, Government House hosted the visit of another Governor General, the Marquis of Lansdowne.

In 1886, when it was rumoured that friends of Cornwall were advocating his reappointment for a second term, the Colonist argued that there was "no act that would entitle him to such an honour", and that five years was "long enough for any one man".[37] Presumably it was early in 1887 when Cornwall was succeeded by Hugh Nelson, recently retired from the management of a lumber mill at Moodyville on Burrard Inlet. He had come from Ireland to British Columbia in 1858, and, like his predecessor, was a Senator at the time of his appointment.

The Nelsons gave their first ball at Government House on 2 November 1887, and the lengthy newspaper account the next day is full of the usual fulsome cliches. While the pace of social life in Victoria quickened during the Nelson regime, the general public's standard of comfort must also have risen, for the Colonist was most critical of the old building:

> The severe weather has severely strained the resources for keeping Government House warm and comfortable. . . . it has never, in its best days, been a comfortable place. . . The wind whistles through numerous cracks and crevices in the walls; the roof leaks in spite of constant patching; cold draughts penetrate all parts. Fires in all the rooms and halls fail to overcome the cold and damp of the atmosphere. In the selection of a site for the gubernatorial mansion all other considerations were sacrificed to view and situation. A little less view and considerably more comfort would have made the House a place that occupants might enter with delight and leave with regret.[38]

A thorough overhaul and a new heating system were recommended. Every year the government had to pay for the cleaning of thirty-four chimneys: ample indication of the want of a "modern means of heating". In the long run it would be cheaper to erect a new building, but, as the Colonist went on

35. Sessional Papers, 1882.
36. Daily Times, 20 July 1952.

37. Colonist, 22 May 1886.
38. Colonist, 18 Jan. 1888.

to say, "the country is not prepared for the expenditure".

On 19 September 1888, Mrs. Nelson gave a garden party for Lady Macdonald which was followed by dancing in the ballroom. The following September, it is recorded, the chatelaine was "At Home", then a popular form of social entertainment. Planned for a Thursday, it was, at the last minute, postponed to Friday 13 September, because fleet manoeuvres had detained Admiral Heneage and his officers. Some 450 guests presented themselves and music was provided by the band of H.M.S. *Swiftsure*. One of the guests was the Honorable Edgar Dewdney, Minister of the Interior and Superintendent General of Indian Affairs, then on an official visit from Ottawa to the scenes of his earlier career. Three years later he was to become the host in the House where he was now guest.

Within three months of this party there was a near tragedy: Government House caught fire. "A telephone message from Government House called the firemen out and set all the bells ringing. The boys made good time in hitching up and the new engine was at the hydrant nearest to the scene in exactly four minutes."[39] Fourteen hundred feet of hose only reached the gate so another 500 feet were sent for and, in the meantime, a bucket brigade was organized. Thanks partly to the speed of the firemen, only $50 worth of damage was done. More hydrants, nearer the house, were requested. City water had been laid on in 1887, but the one-inch pipe was not serviceable as a fire line. Blame for the outbreak was laid on a defective chimney leading from the boiler. This heating system was but newly installed, according to the report of the Chief Commissioner of Lands and Works.

A Gurney hot water furnace has been provided and connected with radiators situated in various rooms and halls. Upon excavating a chamber for the furnace it was discovered that the subsoil drainage of the area immediately about the house centered under the building, where it accumulated rapidly, causing great dampness upon the ground floor. A trench has been excavated through rock to carry off this water, and a stone drain laid.[40]

That same year "a framed and glazed Conservatory" was added to the south side of Government House. Designed by S.G. Burris, it was twenty feet by forty, and heated by an extension of the hot water lines from the house. In November, 1892, the Nelson regime came to an end. Rather than remove or auction his effects, the Lieutenant-Governor made arrangement with the Government whereby, for an allowance of $364.50, his plate, house and table linen remained in the house. Thus, when Edgar Dewdney moved into Government House, its furnishings were in a more satisfactory state than had been the case for any of his predecessors, but there were other problems—notably the plumbing.

As early as April 1879, Richards had complained that "the bottom of the Bath Room at Govt. House leaks as well as the cock of the pipe in the Wash Room the leakage of which are both helping to destroy the said building". While his plea that immediate steps be taken "to remedy these two evils" was not completely ignored, it was not until June 1893, that a complete overhaul of the plumbing was undertaken. For a matter of several weeks, while a new bathroom was being installed, the Dewdneys moved from the House to the "cottage" of J.H. Worlock on Rockland Avenue, thought to be the second house on the east side from the corner at Oak Bay Avenue. During 1896, a subsoil sewerage and irrigation system was installed because the City had refused to furnish sewerage for the residences in the vicinity of Government House.

In August 1895, the Lieutenant-Governor once again vacated Government House, but for a more propitious occasion this time—a visit of the Governor-General, Lord Aberdeen—for which His Honour was reimbursed in the amount of $250. The previous year the Dewdneys had entertained the Aberdeens at Government House but on this second visit the Governor-General took possession

---

39. *Colonist*, 17 Dec. 1889.

40. *Sessional Papers*, 1890.

Front Elevation

Figure 21: The Conservatory, 1888.

of the residence and entertained lavishly. The state ball on 13 November, however, was held at the Menzies Street Drill Hall, for the more than 800 guests could not have been accommodated in the ballroom of the house. "The supper and buffet refreshments were provided from the Government House kitchen under the superintendence of Mr. Aldridge, the chef."[41] One of the last affairs given by the Dewdneys at Government House was a dance in January 1897, in honor of the Bering Sea Claims Commission. In November, Dr. Thomas R. McInnes became the Lieutenant-Governor, and he too entertained Lord and Lady Aberdeen at Government House, in July 1898. In 1899, the Lieutenant Governor's New Year's reception was held in spite of deep snow, snow so deep that "one Englishman marched up to Government House on snow shoes."[42]

Hospitality such as this continued apace until disaster struck on 18 May 1899. The newspaper account of Cary Castle's catastrophic end is graphic:

CAREY CASTLE IN RUINS. — An Early Morning Fire Destross the Lieutenant-Governor's Residence. — Firemen Fight Hard but Save Only Ballroom and Conservatory.

Fanned by a fresh breeze from the south-west, a fire which had evidently been smouldering all night

in the attic of Carey Castle, the picturesque and historic residence of the Lieutenant-Governor of the province, succeeded in completely destroying that building yesterday morning. The whole of the original castle was ruined, all that the fire left standing being the ball and reception room and the conservatory....

It was no surprise to the firemen to receive a call to Government House. They have been there before, not once, but no less than seven times; but on each previous occasion the fire had been discovered before it had made such headway as that of yesterday morning. A defective flue is held responsible for the fire, and the suspicion is well warranted, as all the blazes have started near the chimney leading from the furnace room and in the attic.

Mr. T.R.E. McInnes, the Governor's private secretary, was the first one to discover the fire yesterday morning. He was on his way to breakfast when he heard a crackling noise, as though the whole roof was on fire. Making investigation, he found that the space between the ceiling and roof was in flames, and that already some of the shingles were catching. The alarm was given and the fire department called. Although not slow in moving, Lieutenant-Governor McInnes had to run the gauntlet of falling embers as he passed through the main hallway, the fire having found its way to the shaft which provides light for the corridor inside the main entrance, and was eating its way down into the building. The Lieutenant-Governor, his family and staff immediately set about saving what they could, but already most of the upper portion of the building was enveloped in flames, and it was only possible to save the furniture in the rooms on the main floor. With the exception of his uniform, which was thrown out when the alarm was first given, the Lieutenant-Governor and his family lost all their personal effects, including clothing, jewels and private papers. His Honor places his loss at $3,000....

With the exception of the main entrance and the round tower above it, which were of stone, the building was constructed of wood, with shingle roof and plastered outside walls. It was a veritable fire-trap, and had yesterday's fire broken out before the Governor's family had awakened there is little doubt but that they would have been burned in their beds....[43]

41. *Colonist*, 14 Nov. 1895.

42. *Colonist*, 4 Jan. 1899.

43. *Colonist*, 19 May 1899.

Fortunately the newspaper was incorrect in claiming that the fire had started from a defective flue for, had such been the case, the insurance company could rightly have repudiated the claim. The adjuster's report, however, based on "completed proofs", indicated that the loss was "total" and full payment was made. Unfortunately, only $8,000 insurance was carried on the building and $4,000 on the furnishings, although the inventory value of the latter totalled 10,116.15 (of which only $1,972 was salvaged, the main item having been the dining room table).

By 25 May it was announced that the Green residence on Moss had been secured at a monthly rental of $50.00 and that the Lieutenant-Governor had moved in to await the reconstruction of his residence. As one Vancouver newspaper declared: "This picturesque old pile, of all and no styles of architecture, was one of the most historic as well as one of the oldest residential buildings of British Columbia".[44] The *Colonist* put it more feelingly: "Although a new Government House had long been needed, it seems hard to part with the old one."[45]

---

44. *Province,* 5 November 1900.
45. *Colonist,* 19 May 1899.

CHAPTER FIVE

Cary Castle
Redivivus

FOR MANY MONTHS AFTER THE FIRE, THE BLACK-
ened and picturesque ruin of Cary Castle became a favorite show place for visitors to the capital.
Meanwhile, the government, with $12,000 insur-
ance money in hand, was preparing the terms of an
architectural competition for the new official residence. This means of selecting an architect was
popular at the time (a competition had already been
held in connection with the recently completed
Parliament Buildings). All architects in British
Columbia were invited in a "Notice", dated 31
October 1900, to submit entries, under a *nom de
plume,* to the Chief Commissioner of Lands and
Works. The closing date was 22 December 1900,
and five prizes ranging from $250 to $50 were offered. Since the building was to be erected "near
the site of the old house", competitors were expected "to make themselves thoroughly familiar

with the natural surroundings and characteristics of
the site before sending in their designs." The exterior of the house was to be "plain though dignified,
suitable in every respect to the purpose for which it
is intended and in keeping with the natural beauty
of the site." As for the interior, the instructions
were:

> The general arrangement of the rooms shall be
> with a view to greatest convenience and security
> against fire. It is desirable that the ground floor
> should be so arranged that all the rooms, or as many
> of them as possible, may be, when required, thrown
> open *en suite* with the Ball Room.[1]

The entire cost of the proposed house was not to

1. Lands and Works, *Competition for the Proposed Government
House at Victoria, B.C.,* 1900.

Figure 22: Plan and elevation of 3rd prize winner, Thomas Hooper, 1900.

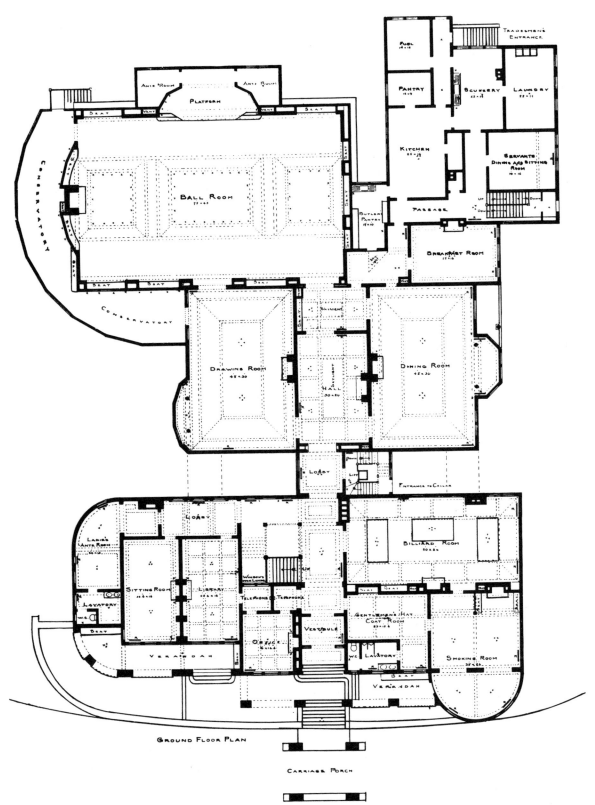

GROUND FLOOR PLAN

CARRIAGE PORCH

Figure 22: Continued.

exceed $50,000. Considering the accommodation desired, the setting of this figure proved an unfortunate error in judgment. It discouraged entrants and, indeed, "not a single architect occupying any leading position in the profession...responded to the invitation."

Two reputable architects, W. Ridgeway-Wilson and J.C. Keith (the latter had already won the competition for Christ Church Cathedral in Victoria), were given the task of judging the entries. A number of the submissions did not conform to the conditions of competition, but were nevertheless considered by the judges. In fact, some of them were included in the five selected designs shown to the public in the Executive Chamber of the Parliament Buildings in the middle of January 1901. The winner of the competition was declared to be Messrs. Byrnes & Tait, of Victoria and Vancouver, under the *nom de plume* "Volute". The other prize winners were R.M. Fripp, F.R.I.B.A., Vancouver ($150); C.J. Soule, Victoria ($125); Parr & Fee, Vancouver ($75); and T. Hooper, Victoria ($50). The judges each received $125 for their services. Actually, the winners had submitted two variations of the same design, Colonial in style. This, as John M. Byrnes explained, was obviously "the most suitable" since it had been used in "most of the finest residences built during this last century."

The winning design was described by the *Colonist* as "plain as a whole" but with beautiful detail, "the subtle grouping of the different masses making a most picturesque, as well as most imposing and dignified building." In its planning, the architects had tried to "cover every want or convenience, without being too lavish", a fault which, said the newspaper, might easily occur in an official building of this description. Nevertheless, the ballroom was to have an organ loft and musicians' balcony—"all of which is cunningly lighted by electricity; also a small spiral staircase, that the musicians need not ascend or descend the grand staircase." The bedrooms had received particular attention:

> They have... been planned with especial regard to the position of the bed, so that the bed is not placed near a window, or in a direct draught between door and fireplace; moreover, the bed is placed so that the sleeper will not have his eyes on the light... Position of doors is carefully considered, that when opened they may shield a greater portion of the room.

A sunken marble bath with three marble steps leading down into it was suggested for the main lavatory. Fire protection was naturally a matter of great concern; a hose-reel was provided on both floors and asbestos board used as sheathing paper. It was pointed out that the house "could be followed out in stone or brick and stone, as easily as wood."[2]

The drawings of this design unfortunately have not survived for our judgment but, at the time, local architects certainly voiced their dissatisfaction. A letter signed "Architect" compared "Volute No. 2" most unfavorably with "Domus Consulis", principally on the grounds that the state rooms could not be thrown open *en suite,* as the competition had required. The government was asked to defer its final decision but was, at the same time, under some pressure to hurry the project along.

> In view of the arrival of the Duke and Duchess of York in... October next, it would be an excellent thing if...the new Government House should be ready for their reception... There is no reason that we are aware of why the work should be delayed. Under normal conditions the time would not be considered long enough... but we suppose it is only a matter of enough men to get the work done in time....[3]

This naive argument was advanced for the equally simple reason that "additional interest would be attached to the structure for all time to come if it was opened for occupation by being used as a temporary home for the Heir Apparent."

The newspaper did admit, however, that "there may be difficulties." There were indeed. Detailed plans were not completed and approved by the cabinet until July 1901, and only then could the

---

2. *Colonist*, 17 Jan. 1901.
3. *Colonist*, 16 Mar. 1901.

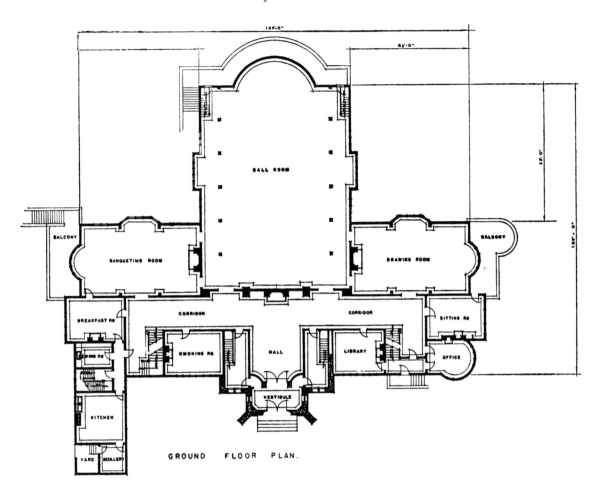

Figure 23: Ground & First floor of Cary Castle, Maclure & Rattenbury.

specifications—without which, of course, it was impossible to call for tenders—be written.[4] The only work that could be done had already been done: the complete removal of the ruin of Cary Castle and the preparation of a new site—near the old one but more conveniently located and with a better view.

There were still further complications for, on 12 September 1901, the newspapers reported the appointments of Samuel Maclure as architect of the new building and of F.M. Rattenbury as supervising architect. This was indeed a surprising turn of events. It was later revealed that the Chief Commissioner of Lands and Works, W.C. Wells, had in August 1901 requested Rattenbury to examine "some plans for Government House" and act in conjunction with the architect who had originally drawn them.[5] Rattenbury refused. He was then asked to prepare his own set of drawings; this too he declined. Wells then appointed him supervising architect, and asked him to nominate a second architect to draw another set of plans. To this suggestion, Rattenbury, who had already, in 1893, won the competition for the design of the Parliament Buildings, consented. He chose Maclure as architect, and agreed to give him an equal share of the fee. Unfortunately, Maclure fell ill and in the end the house seems to be mainly the work of Rattenbury. They must have worked rapidly for, by the end of September 1901, the *Colonist* was able to describe the plans:

The architecture is of a modern school, and novel in

4. *Colonist*, 19 July 1901.

5. *Colonist*, 12 Feb. 1904.

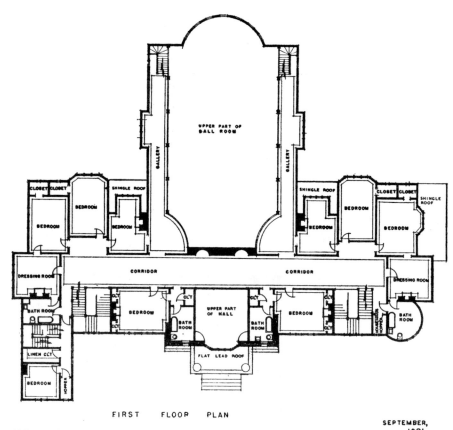

FIRST   FLOOR   PLAN

SEPTEMBER,
1901.

Figure 24: Maclure & Rattenbury design.

effect... The windows are arranged in steps and their arrangement with the castellated cresting and ramparts at the tower tops gives the main entrance indeed a striking castle effect.

The remainder of the building will be of timber, shingled for the most part, and the back of the building, with the walls of the ballroom, which rise from the rocky bluff at the rear, and are only seen from below, will be of cement and iron lathing, resembling stone in effect.[6]

On the basis of the lowest tender, the contract for the construction of the house was awarded to Richard Drake of Victoria for the sum of $44,764.50. C.M. Cookson was awarded the heating contract at $4.975. The total cost of house and furnishings, exclusive of the $12,000 yielded by the insurance policy after the fire, was $111,394.21, somewhat more than the $50,000 original limit.

By the middle of November 1901, ground had

been broken, and the Duke and Duchess of York had come and gone. They had stayed at the Mount Baker Hotel in Oak Bay. Not until April 1903, was the building far enough advanced to warrant mention in the newspapers. At that time the carpenters were completing the interior woodwork, and the decorator was about to begin the "process of interior adornment".[7] The furnishing of the house was well in hand: four carloads of special furniture had arrived from England–three ordered through Weiler Brothers and one through the firm of David Spencer.

When the new Government House was ready for occupancy there was a new Lieutenant-Governor of British Columbia. Lieutenant-Governor McInnes had been living in the Green residence on Moss Street a little more than a year when, in June 1900, he was dismissed from office on constitutional grounds and Sir Henri Joly de Lotbinière appointed

6. *Colonist*, 29 Sept. 1901.

7. *Colonist*, 10 Apr. 1903.

to succeed him. Dr. McInnes was allowed a decent interval in which to vacate the Moss Street house and, until late July, Sir Henri occupied quarters in the Driard Hotel. By the middle of August 1903, apparently with no official ceremony, he moved into Government House, "now rapidly approaching completion".[8]

Shortly after the Lieutenant-Governor took possession of his residence, the building contractors made claims for extra work done and extra materials furnished. The government then appointed a board of arbitration consisting of Thomas Hooper, A. Maxwell Muir and W.T. Dalton. Attached to their appointment notification was a memorandum making certain charges against the conduct of the architects who had been employed. To investigate these allegations, the Legislative Assembly set up a select committee of five members. Rattenbury had already taken strong exception to the allegations and the Committee, after several stormy meetings, reported itself "convinced that Mr. F.M. Rattenbury, as Supervising Architect, thoroughly protected the interests of the Province and that, in all matters brought to its notice, his conduct throughout has been honourable and satisfactory."[9]

While these charges were being investigated by the government, the general public was enjoying the splendors of the new Government House. The furnishings supplied in the temporary official residence on Moss Street had been modest enough. The front hall, for example, contained:[10]

> Brussels Carpet as laid (new)
> 1 Oak Hall Chair
> 1 " Settee
> 1 Large Oak Table
> 4 Oak carved antique chairs covd. in green velvet
> 1 Small Centre Table
> 1 Inlaid Brass Bound Marguerite Table
> 3 arm chairs
> 1 screen
> 2 Pairs Curtains
> 1 Barometer

There was no barometer in the hall of the new Government House but the rest of the furnishings were more opulent:[11]

> Turkey Carpet 23 x 16 x @23/
> Double Ottoman Stuffed Hair and Upholstered
> 4 Chairs in Dark Oak rush seating 30/ea.
> 2 " with arms £2.9.6. ea.
> 2 Wicker work upholstered Derby Chairs 35/ea.
> 2 Upholstered Buxton Chairs 38/ea.
> Antique gate table in dark Oak
> 2 side Tables in dark Oak £1.15.0 ea.
> 2 Large Lounge Chairs, Stuffed hair and upholstered in tapestry £7.5.0 ea.
> 2 Painted Tapestry panels 12 x 20
> 2 Palm Stands in Oak banded with copper £3.0.0. ea.
> 2 Wrought Iron Fire Dogs
> 2 Large Beaten Brass Jardinieres @£5.15.0

The two painted tapestry panels are amusingly described, along with more serious comments on the house in general, in a long article by "M.T." in the *Manitoba Free Press*—surely indicative of the widespread interest, if not the inter-provincial jealousy, which the new building had evoked:

> I believe there is nothing distinctly Elizabethan in the architecture, although I have heard it called Elizabethan. Like the parliament buildings, it is a "free rendering" with Western domestic adaptations. The state apartments of the interior are very handsome, and of imposing proportions. The hall is panelled in oak, with a carved gallery over the hooded red brick mantel opposite the entrance. Here are hanging some oil paintings, of which the Governor is very proud, done by a local artist. Above the oak panelling, at right angles with the gallery, are two very striking canvasses of decorative mural paintings sent out from England as part of Government House furnishings. They are of immense size, and represent British Columbia before and after civilization. At first glance I thought they had been done by the Indians; a second and longer look suggested some ancient Japanese woven tapestry. I thought they were hideous, and I am afraid I think so still, although I know now they are exceedingly clever

8. *Colonist,* 16 Aug. 1903.

9. Legislative Assembly, *Journals,* 1904.

10. Inventory . . . July 10, 1900, Lieutenant-Governor's papers.

11. Inventory of furniture . . . no date, Lieutenant-Governor's papers.

examples of symbolic decorative landscape. I know this because I have since been tutored by a charming artist who took considerable pains to explain the difference between decorative and realistic landscapes. I could see at first they meant something locally historic, but that it was good decorative art — well! I think it would take about a century of study to make me like it . . .

The chief interest of the drawing room is the furniture, over two centuries old, saved from the fire which destroyed Cary Castle, and which had been sent from England to furnish the colonial Government House. That which was sent to match it looks very modern and commonplace.[12]

The general rise in the standard of living is reflected in the furnishings of a typical bedroom in the Government House compared with those listed in the inventory of 1881. There is now a five-foot "Double Italian Brass Bedstead" with a chain spring mattress, two down and feather pillows and a feather bolster; two pairs of linen hemstitched sheets; two pairs of Whitney blankets; a "Thick Eiderdown Quilt" and a bedspread. The marble-topped table in use in 1881 is still listed, but is now called a "toilet set"; the slop bucket and hip bath have disappeared, although the coal scuttle and fire irons remain, supplemented by a "fender". The rep curtains and blinds have been replaced by lined taffeta curtains and "flax casement curtains". Instead of a single "wardrobe" there is now a "stained dull Green Oak suite", consisting of wardrobe, "dressing table with oval mirror & jewel drawers", towel rack, "pedestal and 3 rush seated chairs". On the floor is an Oriental rug.

The inventory from which these details are taken covers only the furniture purchased through Weiler Brothers of Victoria from Messrs. Staynes and Wolfe, 9 Hart Street, Bloomsbury, London. The total cost of this shipment, including duty, packing, freight, and insurance, was $17,615.49. There was, of course, other furniture in Government House thus making the former $4000 insurance coverage completely inadequate. From 1903 onwards, no fewer than eight, and as many as sixteen, companies sold policies to the government, and shared the risk.

Soon after Sir Henri and his wife moved into Government House, Lady Joly organized a Shakespeare Club which, meeting on Monday evenings, soon became "one of the recognized 'taken' dates of the dozen ladies who composed it."[13] However, Lady Joly de Lotbinière had not been many months in Government House when her health began to fail. Sadly, she died within the year. Sir Henri took her body back to Quebec for burial and, after his return to Victoria, lived very quietly for he keenly felt her loss. His daughter, Mrs. Nanton, acted as his chatelaine. Her husband, Major H.C. Nanton of the Royal Engineers, was serving as a staff officer with the forces in South Africa. On one occasion, Sir Henri, however, did give a ball at Government House. It was described as "one of the most brilliant functions that has ever been given in this fair outpost province of ours on the western fringe of the broad Dominion." This time, the most elaborate precautions were taken — once burned, twice shy — and "in the lobbies were seen firemen, electricians, policemen or detectives in private dress, etc., all there to see that nothing untoward happened."[14]

Courtly and kindly though the Lieutenant-Governor was, his main legacy to British Columbia was the number of fine specimen trees which he had planted on the grounds of Government House. He was keenly interested in forestry and conservation and, throughout his career, both wrote and lectured on these subjects. No previous Governor or Lieutenant-Governor had left office with more general goodwill and more sincere public regret than did Sir Henri Joly de Lotbinière.

His successor, James Dunsmuir, was one of the richest men in Canada. Son of the founder of the Dunsmuir coal empire, he was well known in British Columbia for his promotion of the Esquimalt and Nanaimo Railway, and for his term as premier of the province from 1900 to 1902. The appointment as Lieutenant-Governor of a man "actively engaged in large business enterprises {was} something of a novelty in the Dominion, but, it is to be hoped, that

12. Quoted by the *Colonist*, 31 Aug. 1905.

13. *Family Herald and Weekly Star*, 11 Sept. 1901.
14. *Colonist*, 21 Jan. 1906.

Cary Castle after fire (view from the southwest), May 18, 1899.

"Maplehurst" (1937 Blanshard St.), built for Henry Rhodes; another temporary residence.

"Gyppeswyk" (David Spencer house, now Victoria Art Gallery); built for A.A. Green in 1889 and occupied by the Lieutenant-Governor when Cary Castle burned down in 1899.

Cary Castle fire, April 15, 1957.

Cary Castle after fire, April 16, 1957.

Anteroom of the ballroom, Cary Castle.

Old dining room, *photo:* Maclure.

New dining room, May 1959, *photo:* G. Warrington.

Central hallway, May 1959, *photo*: G. Warrington.

Old ballroom.

Ballroom, May 1959, *photo*: G. Warrington.

Destroyed drawing room, *photo:* Maclure.

New drawing room, May 1959, *photo*: G. Warrington.

89

Government House from Fairfield Road, May 1959, *photo:* G. Warrington.

Government House gates.

91

Government House, the drawing room today, *photo:* Philip Graham.

the experiment will result happily", said the Vancouver *News-Advertiser* on 15 May 1906. Its contemporary, *The World,* also welcomed Dunsmuir's "charming and popular wife... who will assist in dispensing the hospitalities of the executive mansion, which his vast wealth will enable him to do in a generous-headed and almost regal manner."[15] Actually, His Honour was a quiet and retiring man; but his American wife was a natural-born hostess whose "grace and cordiality"

had, perhaps, never been surpassed in Victoria.

There was now a large family living at Government House. The Dunsmuirs had two sons and eight daughters. As the youngest was only three years old, a nursery had to be provided in the official residence. The first ball given by the Lieutenant-Governor and Mrs. Dunsmuir, in August 1906, "although of a rather private nature, given in order to entertain the Admiral and officers of the visiting U.S. warships," served also as the coming-

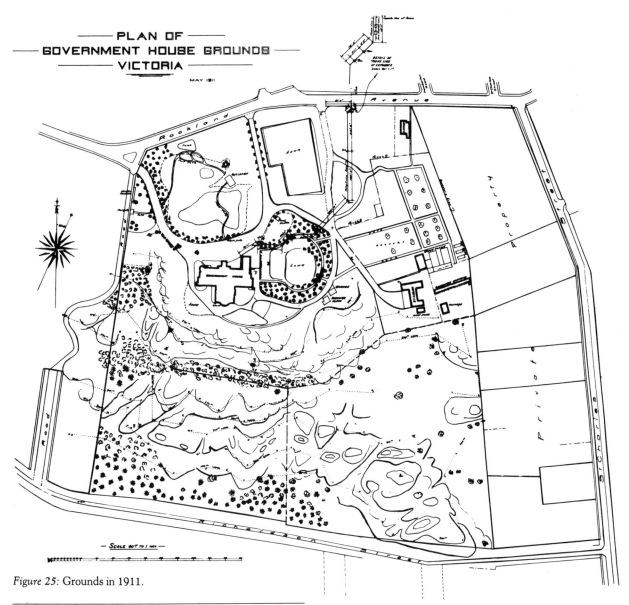

Figure 25: Grounds in 1911.

15. *World,* 12 May 1906.

out party of two of the Dunsmuir daughters.[16] This was a great success and foreshadowed many other equally lavish affairs.

In the spring of 1907, the city began to improve the streets in the neighbourhood of Government House—possibly in anticipation of an increase in the traffic problem if the Lieutenant-Governor continued to entertain on so lavish a scale. One project involved the widening of Belcher Road, or to give it its new name, Rockland Avenue, "to a uniform width of forty feet throughout, instead of having it of various widths at different parts of its course as is now the case." "Without hesitation or demur" the government of the day surrendered "a broad strip of grounds at Government House" for that purpose.[17] Another project was the extension of Richardson Street to St. Charles Street, past the southern boundary of the Government House grounds. The frontage involved was only 630 feet, as Lots 74 and 77 had not yet been acquired, but the government saw no reason why it should contribute even so small a sum as$472.50, spread over ten years, and so informed the city. However, the city put the extension through, and as late as 1917 was still pressing its claim for compensation from the government.[18]

After a relatively brief tenure of office Dunsmuir decided to return to private life and, in December 1909, he resigned. Shortly before his retirement an addition of considerable interest was made to Government House. For over a year Dunsmuir had been planning a new residence for himself on Esquimalt Lagoon, viz., Hatley Park, which Samuel Maclure had been commissioned to design. The drawings submitted to Dunsmuir showed a *porte cochère* which, presumably, so caught his fancy that in November 1908, tenders based on a design drawn by Rattenbury, were opened for a similar porte cochère at Government House. The contract was awarded to Alfred Wood for $3429, a price considered "fair" by the architect, for completion by

15 February 1909. When that date came the structure had not even been commenced for, "in order to avoid undue inconvenience", the contractor had been requested by Mrs. Dunsmuir to wait until he had all the necessary materials in hand. This request, along with wet weather and the employment of too few workmen, to say nothing of the fact that in the interim the architect had decided to lengthen the structure, delayed completion until April, 1909. The porte cochère is still standing. Together with the vestibule to which it is attached —the only surviving portion of the residence erected in 1903—it was incorporated as part of the present Government House.

James Dunsmuir was succeeded by Thomas Wilson Paterson, a Scotsman who had come to Canada in 1855, and been engaged in railroad construction both in Ontario and various parts of British Columbia. He had also served in the British Columbia Legislature from 1902 to 1907. His hobby was agriculture, a fact clearly demonstrated not only by his model farm in Delta but also by the attention which he focussed on the grounds of Government House. Early in his regime he secured the appointment of G.K. Maclean, a Vancouver landscape architect and engineer, to report on the grounds and to "make out a design". The Maclean Report, submitted in July 1911, was the first over-all plan for the gardens of Government House and was accompanied by the map which is illustrated here. One of its major recommendations was the development of a system of driveways and, since Lots 74 and 77 had now been incorporated in the property, two new entrances off Richardson Street were projected. The enlargement of the "small pond" in front of the house was also recommended—if "treated informally, all suggestion of the artificial being carefully avoided". Adjacent to the pond was a site suitable for a tennis court. The old "croquet courts" nearby could readily be improved if attention were given to the proper grading of the "batters" or slopes around them, but "the most prevalent feature of the grounds" was the rocks and a good many suggestions were made for their use "to the best advantage at a very low cost." The common practice of the "piling of boulders and small rocks loosely

16. *Colonist*, 12 Aug. 1906.

17. *Colonist*, 9 Mar. 1907.

18. Except where indicated the details given in the rest of this chapter are drawn from Public Works, file no. 35, Government House, 1905 to 1959 (cited as PW:35).

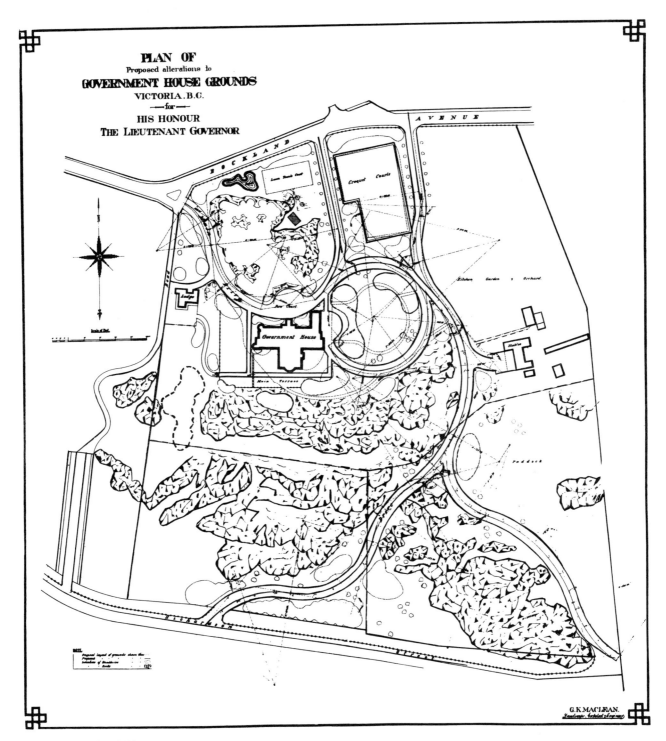

Figure 26: Maclean's Plan, 1911.

on the top of a rock en masse" in a sort of cairn must be avoided for a rock garden "should betray no sign of artifice." Instead, some rocks could be drilled, charged with dynamite, and shattered so as to provide crevices for the roots of plants; in others, larger holes could be blasted in which "large plants and shrubs could be planted so as to throw part of the rock into shade". If water were "carried in concealed pipes, flowing out from underhanging rock, trickling down in a miniature waterfall, and flowing away by a series of rough rock pools", a wider range of plants could be used. Indeed, place could then be found for "an enormous mass of purely herbaceous plants. The tritoma or Red Hot Poker never looks as well as when it can be reflected in water." Recommendations concerning the orchard, vegetable, gardens and paddocks were postponed for the time being but iron fencing along Rockland Avenue was suggested.

Fencing the grounds was of major importance. Practically every year since Kennedy had bought Cary Castle there had been an expenditure for "repairs to fencing". Wandering cattle seem to have done most of the damage. There was also the question of responsibility: who was to keep the fences in repair—the government or the owners of the adjacent properties? In 1877, Lieutenant-Governor Richards, himself a lawyer, had reminded his Attorney-General of the legal problem of liability, "now that the dry season is coming and green grass within the grounds here very inviting to the bands of cattle pasturing in the adjoining land." Richards wondered whether he might impound the trespassers or whether he was obliged to prevent trespass—a problem that could only be resolved by a search of the original conveyances. His language throughout was legal but his problem was distressingly real: the letter ends... "I have a beast in the yard... and do not know what to do with her unless to turn her out to find her back again tomorrow."[19]

After the turn of the century, the district became more urban and the problem of wandering cows was no longer pressing but the old cedar fence was not in keeping with the dignity of the new house.

The Maclean Report recommended that "the main entrance should be as impressive as possible, preferably with rather ornate, wrought iron or bronze gates... with suitable fences carrying out the same effect." Maclean hoped to submit suitable designs for approval and, to that end, conducted a competition among art metal workers. He succeeded in drawing a submission from the firm of William Morris (Ruskin House, London) who suggested "wrot & cast bronze throughout, with vitreous enamelled Coat of Arms". Cost: $8000 for a pair of gates and $5.00 for a linear foot for fencing. Mr. Morris did not get the commission. Indeed, new tenders had soon to be called, because the Minister of Public Works—a new title for, in 1910, the former Lands and Works Department had been divided into two portfolios—had gained the impression that, during his absence and without his consent, Maclean had placed an order for the work with a Vancouver firm. The contract was finally awarded to the Hartley Ornamental Iron & Wire Works of Vancouver, at a prize of $9000 for the main entrance gates and $4 a running foot for the fence. This no doubt appeared to be a relatively straightforward undertaking but it soon became extraordinarily complicated: the size, and even the location of the gates was changed; a number of other alterations were authorized. The contractor was thrown into a state of utter confusion which carried over into his voluminous correspondence with the government. Concerning one invoice, for instance, he wrote:

> This included considerable work that is called "Extra", being an addition to original order, and some of this "Extra" work was gotten in and finished up even before the original contract was anyways near completion. I understand last week that I was getting a *black eye* in the Department for not finishing my contract, but the only thing unfinished was the replacing of the granite blocks in the center of the double gates... with an iron shoe and stop block.[20]

The work was finally completed in 1912, at a cost of approximately $36,000. Hartley had let sub-

---

19. Richards to A.C. Elliott, Richards correspondence, 25 May 1877.

20. PW:35.

contracts for the masonry to John Mortimer & Son, Victoria and to Tiffany Studios, New York, for the bronze work. As a result, his financial affairs soon became so involved that "pressed hard against the wall" he frequently had to plead with the government for money. One such plea, uttered in 1913, "when business ruin stares me in the face", was written, ironically enough, on paper with a magnificent new letterhead containing a half-page photograph of the gates of Government House.

About the same time that the gates were installed, Lotbinière Lane, the western boundary of the Government House property, was paved, the government agreeing to assume one-half of the total cost of $1000. Again it became necessary to consider the problem of fencing. Agreements with the adjoining property owners prohibited the government from building a wooden fence and so stone had to be used. When the tenders came in, the Public Works Engineer pointed out that the cost could be cut in half if prison labour were used, but his suggestion was ignored and the fence was built by contract labour.

Actually, prison labour might well have been used, for prisoners were still brought in to work within the grounds of Government House, a small guard-room being provided for their accommodation. In the opinion of the Warden of the Victoria Gaol, the condition of this building left much to be desired:

> The hut at present is in an awkward position, as it is seen from the Public Road... from the Tennis Courts & other portions of the grounds used by His Honour the Lieut. Governor & his guests, and complaint was made of the disagreeable smells which were prevalent in Summer in the garden from the Toilet Conveniences attached to the Hut.

As the cost of removal and re-erection would be "more than it is worth", the warden recommended its demolition and replacement by a larger structure, since the existing main room provided "very small space for 8 men to feed in, (as it is one man has to feed after others finish)."

The then supervising architect, R. Farror Lawrence, was given the task of designing a new guard house. It was finished in July 1911. Three years later its usefulness was over. In July 1914, the Deputy Minister of Public Works, noting an appropriation of $735.75 for the wages of eleven gardeners, remarked that the "services of the prisoners" could be had, "thus dispensing with some of the paid men". As a means of curtailing expenses this was a vain expectation: in August of that year all the Victoria prisoners were transferred to the new gaol on Wilkinson Road, and were no longer available for work at Government House.

Garden maintenance was indeed becoming a heavy expense. Larger areas planted to garden became practicable when city water was made available in 1887, but the supply was not unlimited and restricted hours for sprinkling were enforced. After visiting installations in California, the Superintendent of Government Grounds, D.D. England, recommended an underground sprinkling system on the theory that one man could then water the whole garden in twenty minutes instead of its taking "half of every day through the season to water an acre of ground, and then would not be done properly". His advice was followed in 1914, although the sprinkler system was not yet on the market and special arrangements for its installation had to be made directly with the inventor. In another effort to reduce expense the old "pony-power" lawn mower was replaced in 1913, by a gasoline-powered machine. There were now two greenhouses and a potting shed in the grounds and, in 1913, a separate heating plant was constructed for these buildings. A constant supply of flowers and vegetables for the House was, of course, one of the major functions of the gardens—a function that was usually well performed. In 1914, however, the criticism was voiced that the new greenhouse supplied fewer flowers than the old. The Superintendent of Grounds replied that there had been "more flowers and plants in the house this past year than in the past three years and of better quality." It was only to be expected, he added, that some flowers would have to be purchased, for "it would be almost impossible to have just what cut flowers are wanted on a certain date not known far enough ahead". The expenditure was modest, not exceeding $100. As for the vegetables, there had been "plenty for the use of the House and to spare" and, he pointed out, the land was "too valuable for the market garden." It is of interest, however, that for some considerable time tobacco was apparently grown in Government House grounds as a crop on which excise was paid.

In December 1914, Lieutenant-Governor Paterson was succeeded by Francis Stillman Barnard who, as a small child, had come with his mother from Ontario to join his father, F.J. Barnard, founder of the Express Company (famous for its freighting service to Cariboo in the gold rush days). Like a number of his predecessors in office, Barnard had been a member of the House of Commons in Ottawa.

The new Lieutenant-Governor and his wife began their duties at a difficult period in British Columbia's history: the country was at war and the normal life of the province was sadly disrupted. The Barnards took an active interest in the House rather than in its grounds. Shortly after they moved in, an inventory of the furnishings was made; "considering the age of the furniture" it appeared to be "in very fair condition". In keeping with changing tastes there had of course been some alterations and additions: there were now lace curtains, maple furniture, and a Heintzman grand piano. The new chatelaine made more changes: she had the sitting room and three bedrooms in the east wing painted white, added new window furnishings and chintz slip covers to these and the drawing room. Outside, "the old stable building", the "coach house used as garage", and the "Chauffeur's quarters" were repaired and painted; the "old closet building" was cleared away and a cowshed and a poultry house were built in the paddock. A new service driveway for heavy trucks was brought into the grounds by the fourth entrance beside the gardener's cottage.

None of these changes were at all complicated, but a request for a change in the "electric light arrangements of Hall and Main Reception rooms... to... a system of indirect lighting from vases and other similar objects" caused considerable difficulty. The Deputy Minister of Public Works had already investigated the situation and was appalled. The electrical arrangements at Government House were, to say the least, astonishing. In accordance with the standard practice of 1902, when the building was wired, the main circuits had all been put in with number eight wire and branch circuits of smaller wire had been taken off without proper fuse protection. Throughout the years the lights had been increased in size and number and the overloaded wires had heated to the point where the rubber insulation was now baked and brittle. Above the ballroom the wires had been "simply laid on the wooden joists and brought out through the ceilings" —and one of the main circuits was carrying a load of 3650 watts through a fuse restricted by the fire underwriters to 660 watts. Once, during a ball in February 1912, "the fuses melted one after another during the evening," alarming the Deputy Minister to the point that, seven months later, he ordered the Public Works engineer to "take special precautions on the occasion of the visit of H.R.H. the Duke of Connaught and immediately afterwards a thorough investigation should be made." His orders were carried out but no action was taken.

In 1915, the period of procrastination was over, but before approving the new Lieutenant-Governor's request for a change in lighting arrangements, the Deputy Minister called for a report from the Provincial Inspector of Electrical Energy. He also secured a report from Hawkins and Hayward who were a local firm of electrical contractors. From the latter the Deputy Minister learned that on several previous occasions, when large scale entertaining had been undertaken, it had been necessary:

> to provide a large fan to blow cold air on the fuses to keep them from over heating. It is necessary at these times to use copper instead of fuse wire in the link fuses to get them to hold, and on one occasion, we found that #10 wire doubled, had been used for this purpose.

The report of the Provincial Inspector pointed out that,

> in several instances the electrical light wires are exposed and are mixed up with bell wires. The main cabinet at the service is made of wood. The fuses are not of the protected type. In the event of a fuse

blowing, molten metal is scattered over the wooden box.

This frightening information produced immediate action. The low tender of Hawkins & Hayward— $4200—for the re-wiring of Government House was accepted, although it had originally been estimated that "probably not less than" $400 would be required." It was hoped that the wiring could be completed during a temporary absence of the Barnards but the work took a month longer than anticipated and a Special Warrant for $600 had therefore to be issued to cover the cost of accommodation at the Empress Hotel for the Lieutenant-Governor. No provision had been made in the estimates for the re-wiring and it had to be covered by another Special Warrant for $6250. This sum also included the cost of a fire-alarm system.

The latter had been installed at the instigation of the Lieutenant-Governor himself who, when the first inkling of the dangerous condition of the wiring reached him, immediately pointed out other unsatisfactory conditions: accumulated rubbish in the basement, and the complete lack of fire-escapes. Called upon for a report on these complaints, the Fire Chief not only confirmed the Lieutenant-Governor's statements but produced his own list of additional hazards: "open joist partitions" without firestops; hot air flues too close to the joists; an ash pit in the coal bin; fire extinguishers that failed to work; no hydrants near the building; and no automatic alarm system. Now thoroughly—and justifiably—aroused, His Honour sent a personal letter to Premier Richard McBride. Noting that the Fire Chief had called the building a "fire trap" he added his own comment:

> That the house has not burned down before this is a piece of good luck and my opinion that it will burn down sooner or later, probably accompanied by loss of life, is a moral certainty unless his recommendations are put into effect.

Barnard apologized for troubling the Premier but felt he was warranted in so doing, "as it may be a matter of life or death." He asked for the immediate appointment of a night watchman—"*and a reliable one*"—noting that Mr. Dunsmuir, "aware of the danger", had employed one throughout his incumbency.

A fortnight later the night watchman was hired. In March the hose at Government House was checked at the city fire hall and "refixed in position same day". By October the Fire Chief had been authorized to install a fire alarm system, including a ten-inch "vibrating gong" on the third floor.

Meanwhile, other, if less vital, alterations were going on apace. Mrs. Barnard had the south and west sides of the summer house closed in with sash doors and casement windows and the cracks between the logs stuffed with moss and covered with bark. The entrance gates and the iron fences were cleaned and repainted. Arrangements had been made with Mary Riter Hamilton to paint a series of portraits, in oil, of all former Governors and Lieutenant-Governors. The intention was to hang them in the Main Hall of Government House but Mrs. Hamilton's commission was cancelled in 1919, before the series was completed. In August 1919, when His Honour was informed of the impending visit of His Royal Highness the Prince of Wales, there was a great flurry of activity. It was customary to paint and renovate Government House for such distinguished visitors and there was little time left. The Prince arrived—to be widely acclaimed by the crowds—and for a few short days enjoyed the hospitality of Government House, an experience which he was to repeat on several subsequent occasions.

The Barnard regime was now nearly over. In December 1919, Sir Frank retired—he had been given the *K.C.M.C.* in 1918. His successor was Colonel Edward Gawler Prior, a merchant prince, a soldier and a politician. A resident of the province since 1873, he had served in the House of Commons in Ottawa where he had the distinction of becoming the first British Columbia member to achieve cabinet rank. He had served also in the Provincial Legislature as a private member, a cabinet minister, and finally as Premier from 1902 to 1903.

Colonel Prior was the eleventh Lieutenant-Governor since Confederation to occupy Government House. Throughout the years the custom had gradually been established that extensive redecoration would be undertaken whenever a new incumbent took up residence, with the occupants being consulted as to the color scheme and fabrics. Lieutenant-Governor and Mrs. Prior were evidently not impressed with the condition of Government House as they found it and they requested the most extensive redecoration. His Honour went so far as to ask for "an allowance for ornaments, etc. for the various Drawing and Sitting rooms as those in use previously were the property of Lady Barnard". The new Supervising Architect, Henry Whittaker, refused this request: "as these items can be purchased at all prices and it is difficult to estimate on what would suit His Honour." Painting and papering was authorized, but only for those rooms which had not been touched for over five years. The tender for this work is of interest: for the first time reference is made to a "Royal Suite", consisting of bedroom, dressing room and bath. The other bedrooms, previously referred to by number, have now become the "White room", the "Yellow room", the "Bachelors room"—a form of nomenclature followed for many years.

The same tender had also included the redecoration of the home of the Private Secretary but only a guess as to cost could be made, as there was "a case of chicken pox there and it was impossible to see the rooms." This house, the original Lodge of Cary Castle, had been converted into a residence for the Private Secretary in 1907, at a cost of $5344.12.[21] Although prior to 1914, a site for a new residence had been allocated and tenders called, the bids were so high that no contract had been awarded and the old reconverted Lodge was still in use in 1920.

Possibly in anticipation of the garden parties she might give, Mrs. Prior now arranged for the furnishing of the summer house. For the most part her plans were unfulfilled for, less than a year after his appointment, Prior died—although not before he had entertained the Duke of Devonshire, Governor-General of Canada. This was the first time that a Lieutenant-Governor had died in office and, as a mark of respect, his body lay in state in the ballroom of Government House on 14 December, 1920.

Walter Cameron Nichol, a prominent journalist,

became the new Lieutenant-Governor. Since the age of 15 he had been associated with the press, beginning with his appointment as a reporter for the Hamilton *Spectator* and ending with his resignation as editor and proprietor of the Vancouver *Province* when he was made Lieutenant-Governor.

The war had come to an end but its impact upon the life of British Columbia remained. New ideas and new influences were at work and life moved at a new tempo—all of which, in a variety of ways, was reflected in Government House. Walter Nichol was a motion picture enthusiast and brought with him "a machine" which necessitated the construction, in 1921, of a "Moving Picture Booth". The installation and operation of this machine caused the Fire Marshal grave concern for the highly inflammable nitrocellulose film added yet another fire hazard to the official residence. The following year saw a request for a "Wine cellar and bath for Chinaman." In 1924 the fence and the gates were again painted and the driveways were hard-surfaced with "Tarvia" (under a contract with the Municipality of Saanich!). The same year saw the installation of an "interphone" system and an electric refrigerator. A vault for His Honour's valuables was also added. A vault in which every brick was "interlaced with an electric current" so that not one could be removed "without cutting a wire, thereby setting off the alarm"—a novel arrangement and no doubt effective so long as it was operated by the electric batteries originally installed, but of "no use" as the chief electrician pointed out to the supervising architect, when it was later "connected to the 110 volt system in the basement... a person can draw the fuse... or cut a wire", and also "it is customary for all power to be off on Sundays for about two hours."

In 1928, an automatic coal stoker was added to the furnace, one of the first such installations in Victoria. The process of modernization and mechanization continued: soon there were purchases of a "flat work ironer", and a dishwasher; a floor polisher was borrowed from the University of British Columbia to be "tried out" in anticipation of a purchase; and the walls of the kitchen and pantry were covered in ceramic tile. A trend is clearly indicated by

---

21. *Sessional Papers*, 1909.

an auction sale in August 1928, when surplus goods from Government House were sold for the net sum of $142.20. No longer was there need for "brass stands . . . wash stands . . . hall stands . . . jardiniere stands" to say nothing of "toilet ware . . . commode . . . meat safe . . . Par([affin] stove".

The age of the interior decorator had now begun and the larger stores all had a "Studio of Interior Decoration". The "bric-a-brac" of an earlier generation was replaced by "accessories" which might or might not be useful. The new and therefore fashionable metal was "oxidized silver". Chintz gave place to plain linen covers, "made very simply", and piped in color. The "doing away with the double beds and have Twin Bedsteads" caused "a shortage of single bed sheets" even in Government House for: "the large sheets will not cut up . . . to advantage as they are the very best Irish Linen costing $70.00 per pair." The fad for bridge and mahjong now called for "cloths" for the card tables. Wallpaper was back in fashion but not without creating new difficulties for the interior decorator:

> This is more or less of a jazz age, which controls to a great extent the style of design and, as one would expect, the colors are vivid and bright, and all papers are very colorful with more or less large floral designs. This treatment of the walls is very effective and very pretty, but we cannot say that it lends dignity, which is so necessary in the rooms for which you require this paper. We have, therefore, made a careful selection of the papers which are going forward to you today and, while they are of the bolder type of design, carry dignity which is necessary in the library. The bedroom papers are more or less of the modern scheme.

This was also an age of contrasts. One Lieutenant-Governor might be annoyed by the cooing of pigeons "roosting about the eaves", and ask to have them shot, while another might be concerned with the creation of a rose garden. The latter was a favorite project of Mrs. Nichol, but the first site she chose was considered unsatisfactory by the gardener and, temporarily at least, the idea was abandoned as being too costly. Nevertheless, before her husband's term of office was over, the rose garden did

become a reality: the old Lodge, residence of the Private Secretary, was torn down and the site adorned with more than two hundred rose plants, a farewell gift to Government House from the retiring chatelaine.

The new Lieutenant-Governor, Robert Randolph Bruce, was a Scot who had initially come to Canada in 1887, and three years later to British Columbia where he acquired extensive mining interests and also large properties in the Windermere District of the Kootenay country. For a short time following his appointment, Government House was without a chatelaine. His Honour was a widower, his wife, Lady Elizabeth Northcote, having died in 1915. In due course, Helen Mackenzie came out from England to assist her uncle and, following her marriage in 1930, her place was taken by her sister Margaret.

The customary renovation of Government House followed Bruce's appointment and a new residence was built for the chauffeur. In 1929, a glassed-in sun-room, ten feet wide, running the full width of the ballroom, with a terrazzo floor which (alone) cost $700 — was erected. According to the Lieutenant-Governor it excited "the admiration of all connected with Government House". The addition had been hurried to completion "in order that it might be ready for use in time for H.R.H. the Duke of Gloucester's arrival on the first of June".

Travel was now becoming easier, not only in British Columbia, but the world over. "The increasing number of visitors from all parts of the world and the necessary entertainment of a great number of these visitors" at Government House was reflected in an increase in the secretarial staff. Indeed, Randolph Bruce himself contributed to this situation: he travelled far more widely throughout the province and attended a far greater number of public functions than had any of his predecessors.

The transition from the lavish hospitality of the "jazz age" to the constricted budget of the depression era was both painful and inexorable. Each succeeding year the appropriation voted for the maintenance of Government House was severely reduced until, by 1933, the allowance was less than half what it had been in 1929. During most of the difficult period, the

Lieutenant-Governor was John Williams Fordham Johnson, who, having come to British Columbia just before the turn of the century in the employ of a bank, was now head of one of the largest commercial enterprises in Vancouver.

While the Fordham Johnsons were in residence, no alterations or additions were made to Government House. Even maintenance work was seriously reduced. A regime which had begun with the delights of a royal visit from His Majesty the King of Siam was soon reduced to suffering such trivial indignities as an extremely shabby and worn hall carpet. The Chief Architect admitted the wear but the $1430 necessary to purchase a replacement was simply not available. The Lieutenant-Governor, fully aware of the "necessity for the strictest economy" and the government's "policy of retrenchment", bowed to the inevitable but not before he had instructed his secretary to write as follows:

> His Honour desired me to say that he would go further than the Chief Architect and would point out that the carpet in question is not only well-worn but is in a condition unfitting it for further use in even a private residence. In Government House, visited as it is by so many representative people of Canada, the British Empire and foreign countries, His Honour feels an atmosphere of decency and dignity should prevail and the presence of this very badly worn carpet in the front hall and its conterminous corridors serves emphatically to convey a precisely opposite and extremely detrimental effect.

Retrenchment there was, but there came the day when Fordham Johnson retired to his Vancouver residence, taking with him all his possessions, and his successor was confronted with a "Governor's suite" in which there was "practically no furniture". Some minor alterations in the House were met by a supplementary vote, but a request for an additional $3000 for furnishings was rejected, the government rather pointedly informing the Public Works Engineer that "any new furnishings ordered and installed by His Honour at his personal expense will, of course, remain his private property and may be removed at the termination of his term of office.

Fortunately, the new appointee, Eric Hamber, was willing to assist the government in this respect.

Slowly but effectively he and his wife set about restoring Government House to the status that years of enforced economy had imperilled. Almost immediately some physical improvements to the House were made: a new telephone system with a private switchboard was installed and the billiard room was converted to a lounge.

In September 1937, Franklin Delano Roosevelt became the first President of the United States to be entertained at Government House. Historic as this event was it was completely overshadowed two years later by the visit of their Majesties King George VI and Queen Elizabeth. Following the announcement of the Royal Visit, there was great activity: samples of new wallpaper came by air from New York; the Department of National Defence provided three sets of blueprints for a "sentry box"; a public address system was installed; new crystal and silver light fixtures were designed and fitted; all the fireplaces were retiled; the insurance coverage was raised; and the whole building was subjected to a rigid inspection by the Fire Marshal. Everything was in readiness when, for the first time in the history of British Columbia, the royal standard of a reigning monarch was broken out over Government House on the evening of 29 May, 1939.

Six months later Canada was at war. Once again, patriotic rather than purely social functions filled the calendar of Government House. Those who remembered the days of the First World War were aware of a difference: in the intervening years, the economy of the province had become much more stable. The threat of bankruptcy, which had been imminent in 1914-1918, no longer faced the people of British Columbia. They were, in fact, about to experience prosperity on an undreamed of scale. A prosperity which, despite war time restrictions, was reflected at Government House. This time, too, the war came closer to home and, in 1941, Government House was prepared for "black-out" and the staff was trained in air raid precautions. Moreover, there was now in residence a Lieutenant-Governor who had personal experience of the hazards of war. William Culham Woodward, while serving with the Department of Munitions and Supply, had been rescued in mid-Atlantic from a torpedoed ship.

Like many other large establishments during the war, Government House soon began to feel the effects of price increases and labour shortages. It became impossible to maintain either the house or grounds at the previous high level, even though the appropriations were increased to the point at which, for the first time in the history of the province, attacks were made in the Legislature upon the very existence of Government House as an institution. In 1943, His Majesty's Loyal Opposition, the CCF party, suggested that the building should be converted into "a home for the aged".[22] The government merely had the roof re-shingled and the west porch glazed. In 1945, the CCF suggested that the House be used "to relieve the shortage of housing accommodation" or as "a tuberculosis hospital". Premier John Hart announced that his "government had no such intention" and doubted that the Opposition had "made the suggestion seriously".[23]

In 1946, Lieutenant-Governor Woodward was succeeded by Charles Arthur Banks and during his regime the utilities at Government House were further improved. A modern laundry was installed; stainless steel sinks and tables were provided for the kitchen, and a new garage was built.

Meanwhile, as a tourist attraction, the popularity of Government House and its gardens had increased beyond all reasonable bounds, threatening to leave His Honour no privacy whatsoever. It was pointed out on the one hand that the grounds were public property; on the other, that they could hardly be considered a public park. Finally a compromise was effected: commissionaires were stationed at the gates and, at specified hours, the gardens were open to foot traffic since it was "not the policy of the Government to have Government House grounds closed to the public".

Because of the demands of his own business affairs, Banks was permitted to retire at the end of the fourth year of his term of office. He was succeeded by Clarence Wallace and, for the first time, a native son of British Columbia was in residence at Government House. He had been born in Vancouver, and at the time of his appointment, in 1950, was president of a large shipbuilding firm there. Soon after his installation an extensive renovation of the House and its furnishings was under way, for the new Lieutenant-Governor was a very popular host and Government House was about to enter upon a period of lavish hospitality.

The following year, in preparation for the visit of Her Royal Highness, the Princess Elizabeth, and her husband, H.R.H. the Duke of Edinburgh, even more extensive alterations were carried out: the complete redecoration of the ballroom, as well as the refurbishing of the other public rooms, the private suite of His Honour and Mrs. Wallace, the Gold Suite, and, of course, the Royal Suite. For these projects Mrs. Wallace secured the services of Jean van Luven, a Vancouver interior decorator, and the cost was covered by a special warrant which, it is interesting to note, was for a sum equal to the vote which in 1865 the Legislature had reluctantly passed for the purchase of Cary Castle—a significant comment on the growth of the province during the 86 years which had intervened.

Although in 1937 Eric Hamber had suggested that the ballroom be redecorated, it had not even been re-touched since 1903—with good reason. The original work had been undertaken by James Bloomfield (later Blomfield), an engraver and a designer who was also responsible for the City of Vancouver coat of arms and, at least in part, for the stained glass windows in the present Parliament Buildings. According to contemporary comment, Bloomfield was "allowed a free hand in the selection of the decorations" for the ballroom and he produced an "historicoethnological plan" based upon "the pictorial records of the British Columbia Indian tribes, the totemic legends, working them up in all sorts of cunning devices." In the spaces between the five arches of the gallery, on each side, he placed the "colossal figure of an Indian warrior, with muscular arms extended. On his breast appears the shield of one of the great tribes, with the armorial bearings copied from the totems of the tribe". Bloomfield based his designs on drawings by "a native Haidah draughtsman and carver", some of whose other drawings had been acquired by the Smithsonian Institution in Washington and the Anthro-

22. *Colonist*, 17 Mar. 1943.
23. *Colonist*, 15 and 16 Mar. 1945.

pological Museum in Berlin. He worked out these conceptions in a riot of *Art Nouveau* style, interlacing the whole room with "a swirl of waves", "pine cones and pine needles", eagles with "wings extended [each] bearing a wreath of oak leaves in its beak", "the dogwood and other characteristic trees of British Columbia", and "the continuous convention of skunk cabbage". The Imperial cypher and the arms of the province, as well as the arms of the Douglas family and of the "house of Joly de Lotbinière" were also incorporated into the design, to produce a "tout ensemble...decidedly picturesque and striking".[24]

This masterpiece of an earlier day was now to be replaced by the white and gold simplicity of a ballroom in which the most striking feature was a pair of Venetian crystal chandeliers. The brilliant elegance of a state ball in such surroundings is easy to imagine; but, during the two days that H.R.H. The Princess Elizabeth and her husband were in residence at Government House, no such function took place. Instead, a private showing of special films was held one evening in the ballroom.

Among the other work done in preparation for the royal visit, and perhaps the most interesting, was the installation of exterior lights "to illuminate the seven leaded windows at the top south end of the Ballroom". Later, in 1953, fixed metal awnings were attached to the lower windows which enclosed the sunroom. That same year a tourist from California "discovered", under numerous layers of paint, the original Tiffany bronze work on the main gates and it was decided to restore them to their original condition.[25] The task of cleaning was laboriously carried out at the Provincial Mental Home at Colquitz, the building originally known as "the new gaol on Wilkinson Road".

In October 1955, the term of office of Lieutenant-Governor Wallace came to an end. As a farewell tribute from the Province, a copy was made of his desk, a great favorite with him and one of the original furnishings of Government House. It was a fortunate choice: within a few years the original desk was to be destroyed by fire but, from this copy, a second copy was to be made for Wallace's successor, Frank Mackenzie Ross, and so another link with the past remained unbroken.

Lieutenant-Governor Ross, a Scottish-born industrialist who had settled in Vancouver, brought to his high office a deep love of his adopted Province. Within the official residence, he made the simple yet imaginative gesture of hanging the walls with paintings of topical interest to British Columbians.

When, in 1900, the replacement for Cary Castle was being planned, an insurance agent writing in the *Colonist* had pointed out the "absurdity" of building in wood instead of stone.

> The idea of building a frame residence for Government house suggests the idea that the members of the government of British Columbia must have been born and brought up in the backwoods and never seen the magnificent houses and castles... built of stone, which lasts for centuries.[26]

His presumption that the wooden house "would only last for some 50 or 60 years" was to be proven correct. Fire was always a threat and a danger. In the beginning defective wiring and inadequate protective equipment created the main risk; then came the hazard of nitro-cellulose film to which, in time, was added the menace of cigars and cigarettes. In the eighteen months preceding February 1954, seven claims "mostly... for cigarette burns" were made on the insurance companies which prompted the Government Insurance and Safety Officer to state "there is... a real risk here not present in most government buildings" as he urged the government to continue its insurance policies and to consider increasing the coverage. A year later, his successor, in support of his recommendation that "coverage by private underwriters be maintained and the Government's policy of self-insurance be not extended to Government House", wrote:

> ... we continually have damages to rugs and furniture from cigar and cigarette burns, consequently there is always considerable risk that sometime a serious fire may result from such carelessness. Also,

24. *Colonist*, 16 Aug. 1903.
25. *Daily Times*, 30 Mar. 1954.

26. *Colonist*, 14 Nov. 1900.

should a major fire occur which would require extensive repairs or replacement of the building, there would not likely be any adverse criticism from any public group if such cost was to be met with insurance monies.[27]

This was sound advice for, within eighteen months, danger had advanced from another quarter. On 1 September 1956, a brush fire in the grounds had threatened to get out of control and, in consequence, the Fire Chief requested that the underbrush be removed, pointing out that there had been "several fire calls for brush and grass fires in Government House grounds". This request was met but not before attention had been called to the deterioration of the firebrick in the furnace and the suggestion made that "the boards adjoining the furnace should be replaced with metal." In January 1957, the Inspector of Electrical Energy suggested improvements in the overloaded wiring system and, in April, when floodlighting of the building was under consideration, the Superintendent of Public Works again advised an "enlargement of the service . . . in order to take care of the electrical load."

Then, on 15 April 1957, the often predicted disaster struck again.

NOTHING SAVED IN DAWN INFERNO

A blast furnace-like fire wiped out B.C.'s historic Government House on Rockland Avenue early today.

Victoria's full fire Department couldn't save the building.

It laid waste to B.C.'s richest residence, thousands of dollars in art treasures, historical relics, precious souvenirs and royal mementos beyond valuation.

There has been no official estimate of damage . . . .

By merest chance it claimed no human life.

It drove Lieutenant-Governor Frank Ross and Mrs. Ross and their household staff into the grounds in nightwear. They saved nothing—even a caged budgie perished . . . .

The fire literally shrugged off tons of water poured on it by over 80 firemen, through a mile and a half of hoses.

Fanned by a brisk morning breeze off the straits, it burned out of control for almost six hours.

Still directing hoses on the blaze at noon, firemen saw only seven chimneys, the shell of one wall, and a tiny portion of one wing, still standing . . . .

It had been dark. But as the spreading flames broke through the roof . . . the building exploded in yellow brilliance.

The sun and flames rose together . . . .

High on Rockland bluff, overlooking south Fairfield, Ross Bay and Juan de Fuca, the beautiful home of the Queen's representative in B.C. since 1904, bloomed like a huge scarlet camelia.

Tall, fire-blackened chimneys and an ornamental battlement rise today above the ashes and charred debris of what was Government House.

A mansion, the pride of this capital and this province, has been lost, and with art treasures and souvenirs of history and tradition which cannot be replaced. The cost . . . in material terms is heavy, in intangibles, immeasurable.

Stately rooms that were never coldly impersonal, that were always blessed with a warm, human graciousness, have gone. This was not merely the official residence of the sovereign's representative in British Columbia. It was home to the men who have held that position . . . . Through the massive oak doors had walked men and women of all degrees, received with a hospitality that brought stature to the province and had won respect, admiration and affection for those who dispensed it.

It is of such things Victorians think today . . . .[28]

27. PW:35.

28. *Daily Times*, 15 and 16 Apr. 1957.

Epilogue

Government House was gone. In 1899 it had "seemed hard to part with the old one" and fifty-eight years later, the same sentiment was expressed with equal truth but deeper poignancy.

In those first unsettled days, Lieutenant-Governor and Mrs. Ross were installed in the viceregal suite of the Empress Hotel. Shortly thereafter, this arrangement was confirmed for the duration of the reconstruction period. Discussion now centred on plans for the new Government House, and a note of urgency was introduced by the forthcoming British Columbia centenary celebrations in 1958, with a projected visit by Her Royal Highness Princess Margaret, sister of the Queen.

Various proposals included moving the site of Government House to the Beacon Hill Park vicinity and transforming Cary Castle grounds into a public park featuring botanical gardens. The Vancouver Chapter of the Architectural Institute of British Columbia argued that a competition should be held for a "modern" design concept. Others suggested the idea of a Government House should be abandoned. In the meantime, the Rosses themselves unearthed a set of the original Maclure and Rattenbury plans to the old house and proposed that a new building should grace the Rockland Avenue site and be modelled as closely as possible on the former residence. In April, speculation ended with

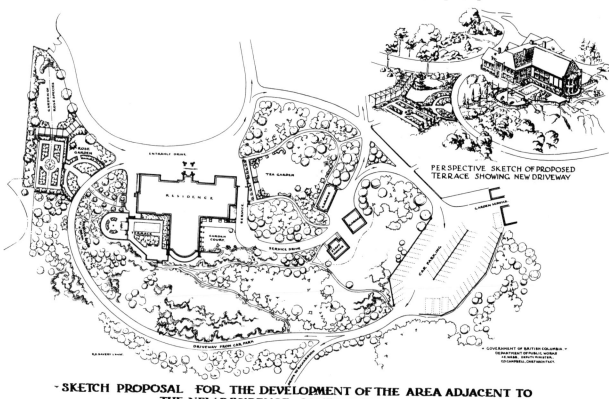

PERSPECTIVE SKETCH OF PROPOSED TERRACE SHOWING NEW DRIVEWAY

· SKETCH PROPOSAL FOR THE DEVELOPMENT OF THE AREA ADJACENT TO THE NEW RESIDENCE GOVERNMENT HOUSE · VICTORIA · B C ·

Figure 27: 1958... Solving the new traffic problem.

the announcement by Premier W.A.C. Bennett that the Department of Public Works would design the new Government House following the design concept of the old former building. Deputy Minister of Public Works and Provincial Chief Architect, C.D. Campbell, was empowered to proceed forthwith.

The final design reflected these instructions. The floor plan followed the Maclure & Rattenbury configuration, although modifications were introduced into the upper storeys. A full basement was added and a double central staircase replaced the former arrangement comprising stairs at either end of the main corridor. The stone porte cochère and tower, left standing at the main entrance after the fire, were incorporated into the new structure. Cost was estimated at $800,000 which did not include furnishings. Minister of Public Works, Chant, claimed

> . . . it will be a dignified blend of the old and new styles of architecture. No attempt has been made to design a contemporary structure, since it was felt that a too-abrupt break with Victoria's historic past would be undesirable . . . the new residence will not occupy much more space than the old one and the general landscaping of the grounds will remain as before.[1]

Response to the final design ranged from fulsome praise to condemnation. Architects were generally opposed. People on the street were pleased that it would not be "one of those new style dwellings with straight up and down lines and a flat roof". Union officials were glad to see construction commence as the project would provide employment during the winter months. In retrospect, the decision was significant in terms of Victoria's urban history as it was the first expression of a new consciousness for the unique architectural heritage and building traditions of British Columbia's capital city. Although many details were significantly different from the old design, it was British Columbia's first major and official monumental "reconstruction", a fact that must be viewed within the context that at the same time plans were under development for the Province's first major historic park at Barkerville.

Excavation of the site began in December. In the meantime, the flag of the Lieutenant-Governor of British Columbia flew over the Empress Hotel throughout the centennial year celebrations. Princess Margaret and her entourage stayed there also during the Royal Visit, the vice regal suite with its entrance hall, drawing room, dining room, master-bedroom and ancilliary rooms for the ladies-in-waiting having been completely redecorated and refurnished under the watchful eyes of Mrs. Ross. The grounds of Government House were used for the garden party on July 14th, and the Royal party

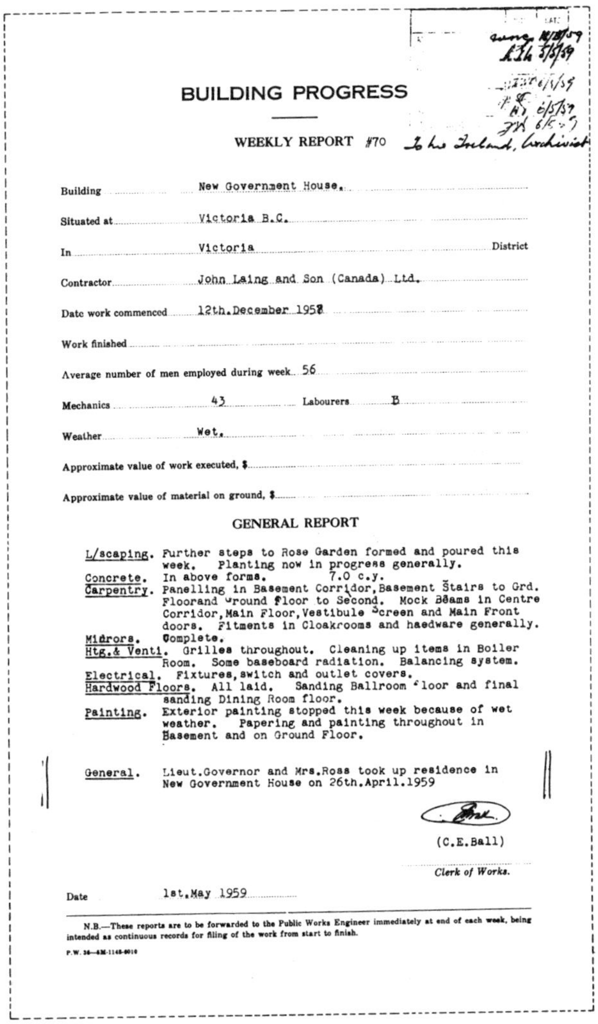

BUILDING PROGRESS

WEEKLY REPORT #70

Building: New Government House.

Situated at: Victoria B.C.

In: Victoria District

Contractor: John Laing and Son (Canada) Ltd.

Date work commenced: 12th.December 1958

Work finished

Average number of men employed during week: 56

Mechanics: 43 Labourers: 13

Weather: Wet.

Approximate value of work executed, $

Approximate value of material on ground, $

GENERAL REPORT

L/scaping. Further steps to Rose Garden formed and poured this week. Planting now in progress generally.
Concrete. In above forms. 7.0 c.y.
Carpentry. Panelling in Basement Corridor, Basement Stairs to Grd. Floorand Ground floor to Second. Mock Beams in Centre Corridor, Main Floor, Vestibule Screen and Main Front doors. Fitments in Cloakrooms and haedware generally.
Mirrors. Complete.
Htg.& Venti. Grilles throughout. Cleaning up items in Boiler Room. Some baseboard radiation. Balancing system.
Electrical. Fixtures, switch and outlet covers.
Hardwood Floors. All laid. Sanding Ballroom floor and final sanding Dining Room floor.
Painting. Exterior painting stopped this week because of wet weather. Papering and painting throughout in Basement and on Ground Floor.

General. Lieut.Governor and Mrs.Ross took up residence in New Government House on 26th.April.1959

(C.E.Ball)
Clerk of Works.

Date: 1st.May 1959

N.B.—These reports are to be forwarded to the Public Works Engineer immediately at end of each week, being intended as continuous records for filing of the work from start to finish.

Figure 28: Progress Report, 1959 . . . occupied but unfinished.

1. Cotton ms. does not give a source. Ed.

were taken on a tour of the grounds, meticulously groomed for the event.

While construction proceeded, plans were underway to solve the age-old problem of furnishings. Over the years resident families had come and gone bringing their own furniture, some leaving pieces behind, so that over fifty years the appointments of old Cary Castle comprised an extremely eclectic collection. The Rosses were determined that a complete and appropriate set of furnishings would grace the new house, furnishings in keeping with the traditional decor and symbolic associations of the building in the political life of the Province. On their visit to Britain in 1957, they personally selected some one hundred and sixty-three pieces of furniture for the new house; many items, such as the

dining room suite, were built to their specifications by the famous Inverness firm of Fraser's, cabinet makers who sent one of its senior employees to accompany the furniture and see it installed. His Honour also commissioned a portrait series of former lieutenant-governors to replace those lost in the fire. On the occasion of the opening of the new house, these, along with a fine collection of Sevres porcelain, sterling silver, crystal and china, were donated to the people of British Columbia to permanently enhance the fabric of Government House. Spurred by this gesture, friends of the Province, both at home and from abroad, as well as many organizations from around the province, offered an array of gifts including furniture, paintings and antiques. The reception and management of these

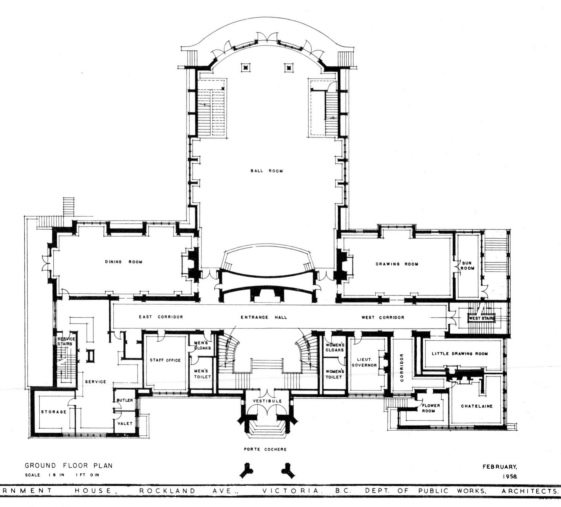

Figure 29: 1959 house. Drawn especially for this book by J.L.S. Wilkinson (con't on p. 109)

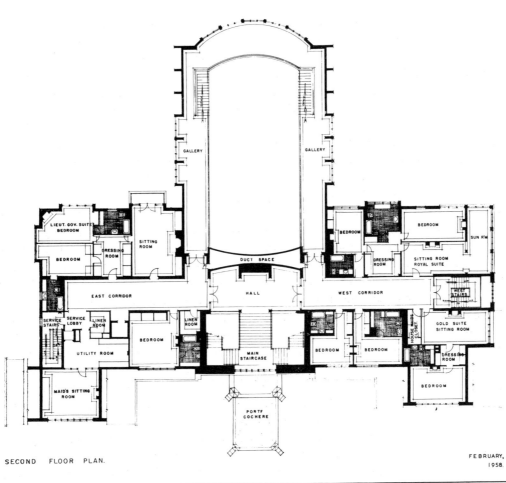

GALLERY   GALLERY

LIEUT. GOV. SUITE
BEDROOM   BEDROOM   BEDROOM   SUN R'M

SITTING
ROOM

DRESSING   DRESSING   SITTING ROOM
BEDROOM   ROOM   ROOM   ROYAL SUITE

DUCT SPACE   WEST
                                                                    STAIRS
EAST CORRIDOR   HALL   WEST CORRIDOR

SERVICE   GOLD SUITE
STAIRS SERVICE LINEN   LINEN   SITTING ROOM
        LOBBY   ROOM   ROOM
                       BEDROOM   BEDROOM   BEDROOM
UTILITY ROOM   MAIN   DRESSING
                               STAIRCASE   ROOM

MAID'S SITTING   BEDROOM
ROOM

PORTE
COCHERE

SECOND   FLOOR   PLAN.   FEBRUARY,
                                                                   1958.

GOVERNMENT   HOUSE ,   ROCKLAND   AVE. ,   VICTORIA.   B.C.   DEPT   OF   PUBLIC   WORKS ,   ARCHITECTS.

items, as well as their placement, was supervised personally by the Rosses.

On April 26, 1959, Lieutenant-Governor Ross, Mrs. Ross, and their staff moved into the mansion. On May 1st, a "housewarming" was held for the more than one thousand people and their families who had planned and built the new Government House. The *Vancouver Sun* noted:

> There is much similarity in the new Government House and the old yet many changes in spacious-ness, light, comfort, colour and modern convenience, planned by a couple who are masters and perfec-tionists at thinking of these happy amenities.[2]

At the official opening ceremony on May 20th, the flag was finally run up a new pole north of the front

2. *Sun*, 22 May 1959.

entrance; this also was a gift from the Ross family. That summer, in July, the Rosses hosted their first official guests, Her Majesty Queen Elizabeth II and Prince Phillip, Duke of Edinburgh. This time the Royal Standard fluttered above the house. In October, Mr. and Mrs. Ross returned to private life, well remembered for their singular contribution to the history of the Province's highest office.

English-born George Randolph Pearkes, V.C., 72, veteran of two World Wars, politician extra-ordinary, long-time Member of Parliament and Tory Defense Minister, succeeded as British Columbia's twentieth Lieutenant-Governor. His wife, Constance Blythe Copeman-Pearkes was born on an Alberta foothills ranch and educated in Victoria and England. Major-General Pearkes took the oath of office on October 13th, 1960.

If the Rosses had concentrated on the physical

reconstruction of Government House, the Pearkes' were to take Government House to the people. No other Lieutenant-Governor had travelled within the Province so extensively, especially among the native people. Receptions, balls, ceremonies and parties at Government House responded to these concerns; invitation lists reflected the demography and geography of the Province. The vice regal couple loved flowers and their attention focused on restoring and enhancing the grounds of Government House. It was General Pearkes' idea to identify parts of the gardens with former chatelaines of the predecessor mansions. Markers in brown hardwood were placed at various points to identify special landscape features and those chatelaines under whose directions the features had been planned and executed. The rocky prominence north of the drive near the main entrance was developed as a native plant garden, featuring flora and fauna from Vancouver Island and alpine varieties from Manning Park on the mainland. This mound became aptly but irreverently known as "Pearkes' Peak" as it was here that Mrs. Pearkes' name was posted. The popularity of the Pearkes during their term of office is reflected in the unusual fact of their being requested to stay on another two years after the usual five-year term of office expired. Thus Lieutenant-Governor Pearkes and Mrs. Pearkes were host to the numerous celebrations that accompanied Canada's centennial of 1967.

At the end of June, 1968, it was announced that John Robertson Nicholson, O.B.E., 66, a silver-haired, six-footer, graduate of Dalhousie University, lawyer, businessman, civil servant and politician would be the next Lieutenant-Governor of British Columbia. His wife was formerly Jean Annand of Halifax. Nicholson lived in Vancouver most of his life but during World War II served as Deputy Comptroller in the Federal Department of Munitions and Supply. John Nicholson was first elected to the Commons in 1962, then again in 1963 when he was appointed Minister of Forestry, later being named Minister of Labour.

Perhaps with a lower profile, the Nicholsons accepted the responsibilities of the office, maintained the traditions, but also inaugurated some innova-

tions. Time-long protocol called for the Lieutenant-Governor to open sittings at the British Columbia legislature and then host a series of State ceremonies following the event. A change in procedure now saw both the Lieutenant-Governor and his chatelaine act as official hosts and receive guests at State dinners and other functions. Similarly, the guest list which was once entirely male, except for female cabinet ministers or members of the legislative assembly, from thence forward included spouses.

Few physical alterations to Government House have marked the more recent regimes. On the retirement of the Honourable Walter S. Owen, Q.C., L.D., in 1978, the major physical change left by Owens was the addition of an outdoor swimming pool overlooking the south slope. The pool is a gift of the Owens' four children in honour of their father's term of office. Throughout these years however, Government House developed as a social and education centre, not only for the political life of the Province but also for British Columbians in general. In recent times over 16,000 people per year have visited the House. They attended luncheons, teas, dinners, receptions, balls, garden parties, performances, presentation ceremonies, and tours. Annually, the House hosts important awards ceremonies for the Queen's Venturers, Dominion of Canada Rifle Association, Duke of Edinburgh Awards, Children's International Summer Villages and Long Service Awards for the Canadian Corps of Commissionaires and the Provincial Public Services, and also the Commonwealth Bravery Awards by the Royal Life Saving Society of Canada. Guided tours are given to school children to afford them a glimpse of the history and role of the Lieutenant-Governor in parliamentary government.

Visiting high commissioners, ambassadors, prime ministers and heads-of-state are regularly entertained at Government House.

The royal family have been frequent visitors to the House: His Royal Highness Prince Phillip in 1978, Prince Andrew in 1977 and 1978 and Prince Charles in 1979 and 1980. Other recent notable guests have been the Governors General of Canada, Jules and Madame Léger in 1976 and 1978 and Edward and Mrs. Schreyer in 1979, also Lord Louis Mountbatten and Lady Brabourne in 1977, Helmut Schmidt, Chancellor of West Germany in 1977 and the Rt. Hon. Kenneth Borthwick, Lord Provost of Edinburgh in 1978.

The many contemporary uses of the new Government House reflect the broadening role of the Lieutenant-Governor and the popularity of recent incumbents. Government House today is the residence of the Queen's representative to the people of British Columbia; it serves as his office and the official centre of hospitality for the Province. The grounds are open to the public and constitute a major recreational asset to the local community.

A scroll bearing the word "Salve", Latin for 'Welcome', surmounts the marble fireplace in the drawing room. This motto is imbedded in the history of British Columbia's vice-regal residence.

BIBLIOGRAPHY

A NOTE ON SOURCES

This account of Government House has been based as far as possible on original documents in the files of the Department of Public Works and the Department of Lands and Forests and in the Provincial Archives of British Columbia. In the Department of Public Works, correspondence and plans have been consulted; in the Department of Lands and Forests, the file of maps; in the Archives, the official despatches to and from the various governors as well as their own semi-official correspondence; the files of the Lands and Works Department (the predecessor of the Department of Public Works), the Attorney General, and the Colonial Secretary; and the extensive collection of maps, plans, and photographs. The memoirs, diaries and letters of private individuals have also proved of value, especially the reminiscences of early Victoria written by James Robert Anderson and by Dr. John Sebastian Helmcken. Use has also been made of two M.A. theses from the University of British Columbia: Lillian Cope's "Colonel Moody and the Royal Engineers in British Columbia," 1940 and Margaret L. McDonald's "New Westminster, 1859-1871," 1947.

Most of Cotton's footnotes have been eliminated; those that remain document substantive quotations which are not sufficiently identified by source within the text. Some quotations used by Cotton were not identified by him and a note to this effect has been given in such cases. A short form of citation has been used which is sufficient for locating the original manuscript or newspaper source.

SELECT BIBLIOGRAPHY

Books and Articles

British Columbia, Legislative Assembly. *Journals* (and *Sessional Papers*), 1872-1874. *Sessional Papers*, 1875. Victoria, 1872.
————. *Papers in Connection with Crown Lands in British Columbia and the Title of the Hudson's Bay Company.* Victoria, 1881.
Dufferin & Ava, the Marchioness of. *My Canadian Journal 1872-8.* London, 1891.
Fawcett, Edgar. *Some Reminiscences of Old Victoria.* Toronto, 1912.

Great Britain, Parliament. *A Further Dispatch Relative to the Proposed Union of British Columbia and Vancouver Island.* London 1886. (Cmd. 3694 1st series).
————. *Further Papers Relative to the Union of British Columbia and Vancouver Island.* London, 1867 (Cmd. 3852, 1st series).
————. *Papers Relative to the Affairs of British Columbia. Parts 1-4.* London, 1859-62 (Cmd. 2476, 2578, 2724, and 2592, 1st series).
————. *Papers Relative to the Proposed Union of British Columbia and Vancouver Island.* London, 1886 (Cmd. 3667, 1st series).
Great Britain, Parliament, House of Commons...*Correspondence between the Chairman of the Hudson's Bay Company and the Secretary of State for the Colonies, Relative to the Colonization of Vancouver's Island.* London, 1849 (H.C. 619).
————.....*Correspondence...on the subject of a Site for the Capital of British Columbia.* London, 1868 (H.C. 483).
Great Britain, Parliament, House of Commons, Select Committee on the Hudson's Bay Company. *Report.* London, 1857 (H.C. 224 and 260; H.L. 197).
Ireland, Willard E. "The Appointment of Governor Blanshard," *British Columbia Historical Quarterly,* Vol. 8 July 1944, pp. 213-26.
Ireland, Willard E., ed. "First Impressions: Letter of Colonel Richard Clement Moody, R.E., to Arthur Blackwood, February 1, 1859." *British Columbia Historical Quarterly,* Vol. 15, January-April, 1951, pp. 85-107.
Jackman, S.W. *The Men of Cary Castle.* Victoria, 1972.
Lamb, J.W. Kaye. "The Governorship of Richard Blanshard." *British Columbia Historical Quarterly,* Vol. 14, January-April, 1950, pp. 1-40.
Nesbitt, James K. *Album of Victoria Old Homes and Families.* Victoria, 1956.
Ormsby, Margaret A. *British Columbia: A History.* Toronto, 1958.
Sage, Walter N. *Sir James Douglas and British Columbia.* Toronto, 1930 (University of Toronto Studies, History and Economics).
Scholefield, E.O.S., and Howay, F.W. *British Columbia from the Earliest Times to the Present.* Vancouver, 1914. 4 Vols.

Segger, M. & D. Franklin. *Victoria: A Primer for Regional History in Architecture.* New York & Victoria, 1979.

Segger, M., ed. *The British Columbia Parliament Buildings.* Vancouver, 1979.

Vancouver Island, House of Assembly...*Correspondence Book August 12, 1856, to July 6th, 1859.* Ed. E.O.S. Scholefield. Victoria, 1918. (Archives of British Columbia, Memoir No. 4.)

_____. *Minutes...August 12th, 1856 to September 25th, 1858.* Ed. E.O.S. Scholefield, Victoria, 1918. (Archives of British Columbia, memoir No. 3.)

Vancouver Island, House of Assembly, Select Committee on Crown Lands, 1863. *Report.* Victoria, 1864.

Vancouver Island, Legislative Council. *Minutes commencing August 30th, 1851 and Terminating...February 6th, 1861.* Ed. E.O.S. Scholefield. Victoria, 1918. (Archives of British Columbia, Memoir No. 2.)

Newspapers

British Columbian, New Westminster.
Daily Chronicle, Victoria.
Daily (British) Colonist, Victoria.
(Daily) Victoria Gazette, Victoria.
Mainland Guardian, New Westminster.
Times, Victoria.
Manitoba Free Press, Winnipeg.
News-Advertiser, Vancouver.
The World, Vancouver.

INDEX